THROUGH
MOSES
TO JESUS

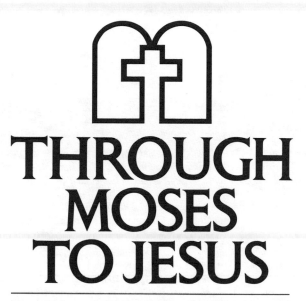

THROUGH MOSES TO JESUS

The Way of the Paschal Mystery

CARLO M. MARTINI, SJ

AVE MARIA PRESS
Notre Dame, IN 46556

Translated by
Sister Mary Theresilde Skerry,
Holy Spirit Adoration Sister

Permissions:

Excerpts from THE NEW JERUSALEM BIBLE, copyright © 1985 by Darton, Longman & Todd, Ltd. and Doubleday & Company, Inc. Reprinted by permission of the publisher.

Excerpts from the English translation of *The Roman Missal* ©1973, International Committee on English in the Liturgy, Inc. All rights reserved.

This book owes its origin to an eight-day retreat given by Carlo Martini to a group of priests in northern Italy in August 1978. The taped talks were transcribed and originally published by Centrum Ignatianum Spiritualitatis in Rome (1979) and later by Edizioni Borla. This English edition is a translation of *Vita di Mose, Vita di Gesu, Esistenza Pasquale*, Edizioni Borla, Rome, fourth edition, 1984.

© Copyright 1988 by Ave Maria Press, Notre Dame, Indiana 46556

Library of Congress Catalog Card Number: 87-73072

International Standard Book Number: 0-87793-375-8

Cover design: Elizabeth J. French

Printed and bound in the United States of America.

Contents

Foreword[1]

In the history of Moses, as in the other events recorded in the Bible, we find realities that are repeated in the life of every individual. Anyone who is inwardly open and acquainted with prayer can find in the words of scripture what is needed for his or her life. It seems to me that the decisive questions to be asked by each person are: What does this scripture passage mean to me? What is it saying to me? How is it related to my life? We might at first say, "It doesn't have anything to do with my life." But rather than remain with such a first impression, we should look for the cause and ask, "Why is there no connection between this bible passage and my life? What would I want the connection to be?" In this way even a negative first impression can be a means of contact between what the Bible says and what we experience. Often this contact does not take place immediately, but only after we have entered into a dialogue, a wrestling with the words of scripture. Only then does it begin to shed light.

Such a dialogue is a decisive help toward prayer, which springs from our center and expresses our deepest yearnings. This is the aim of spiritual guidance: To help us express ourselves in prayer as we are, in keeping with our situation and nature.

Real prayer is not child's play. Scripture teaches us that prayer is a struggle, a battle. It places us face to face with our greatest difficulties. In prayer we are trained to look at the prob-

---

1 The Foreword to this edition is a translation from German of the Foreword to the German edition (Herder).

lems of our life with an open eye and to accept them, for human beings are often afraid to confront themselves.

This book attempts to answer the question of how faith can be lived in today's particular situation. The world, especially our Western world, is permeated with an atmosphere of pessimism. Faith is a leap of trust—trust in the love of God who comes to meet us. This leap is difficult because it requires overcoming the spontaneous mistrust to which we are educated nowadays in more or less every area. But in St. John's gospel Jesus says,

"You will come to know the truth,
and the truth will set you free" (Jn 8:32).

Thus it is only in making the leap that we will experience what faith really does for us and how it fills our hearts.

May this book give its readers courage to dare the leap of trust, so that their own lives may be marked by the paschal experience of following in the footsteps of Moses and of him whom he prefigured, Jesus.

Introduction

Since we want to begin this series of reflections calmly, let us enter it with small steps.

In this first encounter I shall briefly indicate the theme that we are going to consider and the reason for this choice. In addition I will suggest some spiritual reading as a help for us all in progressively assuming a rhythm of life that will serve the spiritual search in which we are engaged.

Moses and Ourselves in the Life of the Church

Moses is a man who lived a history of salvation; he himself followed a certain path and caused his people to do the same. We too are in the course of a journey, of setting out from a certain point in order to reach another.

Moses symbolizes the journey in which the church places the central moment of her baptismal memory, the journey that we all travel anew in the Easter Vigil, in the night of the church, the night of the Christian, the night in which we pass through the Sea of Reeds—the night of our baptism, of our conversion, of our first step forward toward the Lord. In contemplating Moses we meditate on the church's baptismal memory, the source of the entire liturgy, which originated in the Easter Vigil and culminates in the Eucharist. In this memorial celebration of passing through the Sea of Reeds we see Christ's passage through the grave to the resurrection and our own passage from death to life.

The New Testament too confirms the centrality of this theme. In mentioning Moses over 80 times it shows how present he was to the ancient Christian writers, above all as a type of Jesus. At Jesus' transfiguration Moses appears along with Elijah. Moses

9

indeed is a key figure. Together with Elijah he is the point of departure for understanding Jesus.

Outside the New Testament, in the primitive church, in the Fathers of the church, and in the synagogue and its liturgy, we possess a mighty storehouse of the memory of the people of God from which we can still draw profit today.

Let us take a brief look at how the early church spoke of Moses. In passing, as it were, I mention the citations of Justin in his *First Apology* and in the *Dialogue*, as well as the *Letter to Barnabas* where Moses is frequently mentioned. Worthy of special note is the great Gregory of Nyssa who in his work *De vita Moysis* devoted a whole book to the life of Moses. Gregory is one of the classical authors of the patristic literature, so much so that Henri de Lubac and Jean Danielou initiated their famous "Sources Chretiennes" in 1943 with the Life of Moses, subtitled, "Treatise on Perfection in Virtue." Moses is presented as the model of Christian perfection. The book is divided into two parts. In the first the story is related according to the Bible with the addition of some rather imaginative details from various traditions. The second part, containing the theory, considers Moses' significance for the Christian life according to the interpretation of the Eastern Fathers. In this longer part the whole story of Moses is interpreted as applying to Christianity, even to saying that we are Moses, you are Moses. This is the attitude we should have as we enter this series of reflections: I am Moses.

Moses and the Jewish Tradition

Philo, an illustrious Jewish predecessor of Gregory of Nyssa, wrote a life of Moses in which he drew on all the traditions. For the Greeks he presents Moses as the greatest philosopher who lived before Plato and before Homer, as the man who passed unperturbed through the storms of life.

The rabbinic tradition too speaks much of Moses, especially after Jesus' time. Moses increasingly became the representative of the rabbinism that survived the destruction of the Temple.

The entire modern Hebrew tradition lives on Moses. There are very beautiful midrash reinterpretations that deal with Moses with much love, describing him in short stories that, although they might make us smile, contain a very deep pedagogy. We shall cite some of them in this book. These fictional stories about Moses transmit a treasure of human and religious wisdom.

These traditions use a free style; little importance is given to whether the events related actually happened or not. The traditions are concerned merely with what the stories mean for human life. This holds true for midrash, as well as for Gregory and Philo, and it also holds good for us. In the following reflections I too shall use a bit of the midrash style; that is, not everything I say appears in the Bible literally. But following in the footsteps of these grand predecessors, we shall ask ourselves: What was Moses thinking at this specific point in his life? What were his difficulties and problems? and so forth.

Moses Helps Us to Understand Jesus Better

Now we come to the theme of these reflections: the life of Moses, the life of Jesus, and the paschal dimension of our life. These are the three levels of our meditations. We are not searching into Moses' life as such, but are interested in it only insofar as it helps us to understand Jesus' life and the paschal experience of the Christian. This statement could readily recall another from the *Spiritual Exercises* of St. Ignatius in the meditation on the kingdom: "The call of the earthly king helps us to contemplate the life of the eternal King" (91). In our case, contemplating the life of Moses should help us to contemplate the life of the eternal king, Jesus, and our life in him. Thus we shall not treat of everything that could be said about Moses. For instance, we shall not deal with him as legislator, as he is most often regarded and cited, nor as priest or man of the covenant. We shall leave all these aspects aside.

Philo begins his work by saying: "I have conceived the plan

11

of writing the life of Moses, who is regarded now as legislator of the Jews, now as interpreter of the holy law, now as an excellent and perfect man in every respect." What especially interested Philo was Moses the legislator. Gregory, however, writes at the beginning of his book that it is very beautiful to meditate on our patriarchs in order to learn the way of virtue; therefore, he continues, "we shall content ourselves with recalling the life of this illustrious personage [Moses], so that he may do us the service of showing us how it is possible to make the soul arrive at the peaceful port of virtue where it is no longer exposed to the tempests of life and no longer risks suffering shipwreck in the abyss of sin." For Gregory, Moses is the man who knew how to steer through the vicissitudes of the world to the perfection of life. (I seem to see a certain Stoic influence expressed here.) This more specifically historical, salvific aspect of Moses — Moses, the man of the Pasch—is what interests us.

What does it mean to say "man of the Pasch"? It means a man of passage, a man who himself has passed from one experience to another in his life, amid great sorrow and really upsetting events, and has also made his people pass from one way of life to another, a man who throughout his entire life was bound to the initiative of God's passage, God's Pasch. Hence Moses, the man of the Pasch, will likewise help us to understand Jesus, our Pasch, who for us passed through death in order to make us too pass through it and to be our Pasch of the resurrection. Moses will help us to understand Christian life as a paschal life, as the life of those who by the grace of God can sing the song of Moses on the shores of the Sea of Reeds: "God has saved us. He has brought us out of slavery to Pharaoh into the freedom of a promised land."

Meditating on the Revealed Word

Our method will be very informal — to propose some simple reflections, *lectiones divinae*, from a few pages of scripture, above all from Exodus and Numbers, to be read in the light of the New Testament, in order to better comprehend the life of Jesus and the paschal life of the Christian. The basic text to keep in mind in this undertaking of ours is 1 Corinthians 10:1-2:

> I want you to be quite certain, brothers, that our ancestors all had the cloud over them and all passed through the sea. In the cloud and in the sea they were all baptized into Moses.

We shall view the salvation history into which we all have passed, for—as the refrain of the *Haggadah* of the Pasch, the Hebrew ceremony for the paschal meal, says—we too were there with our ancestors, there at the Sea of Reeds; we too were there, we too have passed through. And if we are here today to celebrate the Pasch, it is because we were also with Moses.

It is in this spirit that we shall read our selected texts because, as Paul says, this happened as a lesson for us. Since it has been put into writing, it is destined to be of service to us.

What are the texts? I shall indicate them as we proceed. For now I shall merely say that I have selected the principal texts about Moses from all the traditions, omitting however all the legislative passages.

In concluding this brief Introduction, I cite a passage from Gregory of Nyssa:

> It requires an attentive meditation, a penetrating view, in order to discern beyond the letter of the story what the Chaldeans and Egyptians are that we have to leave. And when we have escaped from this Babylonian captivity, we can enter into blessed life.

First Meditation

The Three Periods in the Life of Moses

Before beginning this meditation, I suggest that you ask yourself this question: Where am I? That is to say, In what situation do I find myself and what characterizes my present situation? This is the question that ought to arise on reading the passages that I shall now propose.

A Division Already Found in Scripture

Our starting point is a text from the Acts of the Apostles in which the so-called three periods in the life of Moses are stated and identified (Acts 7:20-43).

Before this, Israel's tradition had already divided Moses' life into three periods of 40 years each. With scripture's typical preference for symbolism, the events are presented within the framework of three great, complete periods. It is an idea which will be commonly repeated in the living memory of Israel which is the rabbinic tradition.

The following quotation is taken from a midrash in connection with Deuteronomy 34:7. This passage mentions that Moses was 120 years old when he died, and the commentary on this runs:

> He was one of the four who lived to be 120. They are Hillel the Elder, Rabban Johnathan Ben Zakai and Rabbi Akiba.

Moses is the fourth. Then the rabbinic text continues:

> Moses spent forty years in Egypt: then he lived forty years
> in Midian and served Israel for another forty years. Hillel
> the Elder came to Babylonia at the age of forty, served the
> sages for forty years and then Israel for forty years. Rab-
> ban Johnathan Ben Zakai was occupied with the affairs of
> this world for forty years, served the sages for forty years
> and served Israel for another forty years. Rabbi Akiba be-
> gan to learn the Torah at the age of forty years, served the
> sages for forty years and then served Israel for forty years.

We can notice the typical, schematic manner of dividing the life of these four great men into periods of 40 years each. The Acts of the Apostles (7:20 ff.) does the same thing where it presents Moses' life in Stephen's discourse. Our synopsis begins with verse 23: "At the age of forty, he decided to visit *his kinsmen, the Israelites.*" Then in verse 30 we read: "When forty years were fulfilled, *in the desert near Mount Sinai an angel appeared to him in flame blazing from a bush* that was on fire." These, therefore, are the three periods of Moses' life: For the first 40 years, Moses was in the school of Pharaoh; in the second period of 40 years, he decides to visit his brothers and flees into the desert; the third stretch of 40 years begins with the burning bush and lasts until the end of his life. This is the comprehensive outline of Moses' life.

Now let us try to take an overview of the life of Moses and investigate the meaning of these three sections spoken of in the Acts of the Apostles and referred to in the rabbinic texts in connection with other great men of Israel.

As meditation I propose a simple reading of the passage of Acts in which the three life periods are successively described.

1. God Prepares Moses for a Special Mission

It was at this time that Moses was born, *a fine child* before God. He was looked after for *three months* in his father's house, and after he had been exposed, *Pharaoh's daughter adopted* him and brought him up *like a son*. So Moses was taught all the wisdom of the Egyptians and became a man with power both in his speech and in his actions (Acts 7:20-22).

What is characteristic of this first period of Moses' life as described in the Acts of the Apostles in abbreviated form and in the second chapter of Exodus in more detail? Drawing on the passages cited, I would outline this period as follows: First, Moses is the object of God's special providence; and second, Moses receives a choice education. That is the sense of these verses.

Moses is the object of God's special providence in that God saves him. That is the meaning of the story of Moses' childhood. He is in danger of death; he is supposed to be killed; the waters of the river would have swallowed him up, but instead he is saved. A select education is given him: "He was taught all the wisdom of the Egyptians." That is, he was subject to the systematic, methodical initiation and instruction that constituted the model of education at that time.

We know what the wisdom of the Egyptians meant in the world of those days. It was the great wisdom, the proverbial wisdom, the most ancient wisdom, so much so that the Greeks attended the Egyptian schools to capture their secrets. *All* the wisdom of the Egyptians included the political wisdom of an excellently organized empire; the economic wisdom of a grand social and commercial structure; the technical wisdom of the pyramids and of the art of constructing immense buildings and formidable temples; and finally, the cultural wisdom manifested in extreme refinement of life. According to the text, Moses was introduced into all this richness of human culture.

17

After having thus briefly seen what this first stage of Moses' life meant for him, let us now ask ourselves whether we can identify with him and say something similar about our own life, about the Moses we are. I think that each of us can testify to God's special providence in our life. We would not be able to reflect tranquilly on these things except by the special providence of God, who has led us to this moment.

During our meditation, we can reflect with admiration, praise and thanksgiving for this special providence that has saved us from dangerous waters. Where would we be now if the Lord had not held his protecting hand over us? Where would we have ended up? Besides, each one of us is debtor to a tradition of education, dignity and culture. We need only think of the millions of men and women in the world who can scarcely distinguish right from left, who are deprived of the least cultural horizon, and then we can appreciate our privileged position.

Mighty in Word and Deed

So here we are like Moses. And the result? Moses "became a man with power both in his speech and in his actions" (Acts 7:22). Moses knew how to speak and act, and no doubt was very aware of this ability. He knew that he knew; he was conscious of having had a privileged education. Note here the partly christological reference in the text. Jesus is described as being "powerful in action and speech" (Lk 24:19). Moses, however, is mighty "in his speech and in his actions." Moses knew how to talk, and then he also knew how to act.

How should we interpret all this in terms of our life? I think that for each one of us there is a time of formation and preparation in which we learn how to do things. I call this "the time of acquiring methods." We learn how to study, to express ourselves, to develop our own profession, to meditate, to pray. As a result, we form a certain idea of how things are done. This becomes evident in our criticism of others. We think they have not done things right; we would do otherwise under the given circumstances, because we would apply our own methods; we know how it should be done, and so on.

All of us, in varying degrees, have passed through this period in which we believe we have learned many things such as how to deal with individuals, groups and various classes of men and women, and how to handle certain difficult situations. This period corresponds to the initial phase of Moses' education in which he rightly believes in his knowledge of what is to be done or said.

It is typical in this first stage to see things from the point of view of the theories to which we have subscribed, the ideology which we have instinctively made our own. We are not equal to reality as it is; rather, we automatically avoid facing reality. We come into contact not with reality as it is, but with the images we have of reality on the basis of our ideology, our theories and the notions we have learned or imagined about reality. In practice we flee from the truth, even while claiming to be honest and upright, because we are actually seeing everything through the eyes of method or theory, ideology and the options that we deem to be just, good, holy, spiritual, true, and so forth.

All this is characteristic of the first stage of Moses' life. He is too educated. He knows all the wisdom of the Egyptians and judges everything according to it; instinctively, without his realizing it, he lets everything pass through the filter of this wisdom. He is in minimal contact with reality. Hence he experiences anger and disillusionment when the reality is different from what he had thought it to be, different from what he had learned in an environment saturated with ideas.

2. A Period of Generosity and of Failure

Now for the second period in Moses' life. I called the first 40 years a time of acquiring methods and would define the second one as "a period of generosity and failure" or "a time of endeavor and of frustration." Generosity means that Moses is full of good will; he gives of himself to the utmost, magnificently.

> At the age of forty he decided to visit *his kinsmen, the Israelites*. When he saw one of them being ill-treated he went to his defence and rescued the man by *killing the Egyptian*. He thought his brothers would realise that through him God would liberate them, but they did not. The next day, when he came across some of them fighting, he tried to reconcile them, and said, "Friends, you are brothers; why are you hurting each other?" But *the man who was attacking his kinsman* pushed him aside, saying, *"And who appointed you to be prince over us and judge? Do you intend to kill me as you killed the Egyptian yesterday?"* Moses fled when he heard this and *he went to dwell in the land of Midian*, where he fathered two sons (Acts 7:23-29).

Here is the second period of Moses' life, the time of generosity and failure, of endeavor and frustrations. Moses is full of great ideas and wants to accomplish something grand and generous. And in fact, what he does is truly great. Instead of enjoying the privileges that are his by virtue of his belonging to Pharaoh's household, he courageously gives of himself for his people. As a magnificent result of his education, he manifests the courage to fight for justice. Moses cannot tolerate injustice and goes so far as to invest himself by killing the Egyptian. We should note that his endeavor is not a naive rushing into the battle for justice, but is instead supported by clear and valid motives.

Moses is not an anarchistic revolutionary. His goal is very precise — to restore unity among his people, to make them free and to regain for them their dignity. This is what he says immediately on seeing them quarreling: "You are one people; follow me. I will lead you to a marvelous experience which you have never had before, that of being aware and worthy of your ancestry. I know what it means to be free, to love one another." This Moses is magnificent and animated with such high ideals—love for the people and the desire for reconciliation. Moses has in mind not a purely destructive fight for justice but a constructive one.

However, There Is a "But . . ."

In spite of all this, there is a "but," well-expressed in Acts 7:25. "He thought . . . but they did not." He was mistaken; he had conceived a simplistic idea of reality, an idea of his own making, his own ideology. His scheme was very simple: "I, Moses, have been educated in freedom; I know what freedom means. So I will go to my people and propose this liberty to them. I will pay the price of this freedom, and they will understand what freedom means. They will acclaim me as their leader, and we will all march together." *But* . . . all this was only a plan, an idea.

What was it about this plan that did not function? Moses had no realistic idea of the resistance that his people would raise to the summons to freedom. It had not entered his mind or his logical planning. Hence failure was inevitable. Verses 27-29 marvelously describe the total collapse of Moses, a man who with immense generosity had renounced all privileges in order to be poor with the poor, oppressed with the oppressed. The Bible describes with finesse the fiasco that Moses experiences at the hands of his people. They not only refuse to recognize him, but also react: "Who ever told you to bother about us? We're not interested." Thus he is clearly rejected by those whom he intended to teach, those to whom he wanted to bring the right way of thinking.

There is also failure in his confrontation with Pharaoh. He has severed all connection and now he fears that Pharaoh will look for him. Finally, there is the failure of his own person: Moses is a nobody now. The courageous Moses has become fearful. He who was ready to risk his life is now saving his own skin; he has really lost his head; he wants only to get away as soon as possible. The prototype of dedication to others is now

21

concerned only about himself. He flees to a strange land, and we know what being a stranger means in the ancient Oriental world. It means to lose all human rights because the stranger, being among people with whom he has no intimate ties, has no one to avenge him. He is at the mercy of all; he no longer has any rights.

Moses, having left a privileged position, one which he voluntarily renounced to share in the life and destiny of his people, is now ostracized, rejected by his own people. From now on Moses is nothing but an impoverished, frightened man, startled at every rustling of the leaves at night and in the desert. This is what has become of the courageous fellow who knew it all, who had learned the methods and was, therefore, powerful in word and deed.

The final verse of our text shows us another very interesting detail: "Moses fled when he heard this, and *he went to dwell in the land of Midian*, where he fathered two sons" (Acts 7:29). Here we can ask ourselves what his having two sons has to do with all this. How is it that Acts, which so well describes the scene with such pertinent elements, adds this fact that he had two sons? I have the impression that the text wants to indicate that Moses settled down and said to himself: "I've had enough of big ideas and big undertakings, enough of politics! All my dreams of being a liberator are finished. I too have a right to my own life." Moses wanted to look for a quiet little place where he could forget the past and those bitter experiences that he had never thought would happen to him. So much for the second period of Moses' life.

3. God Breaks Into Moses' Life

Now the third stage of Moses' life begins:

> When forty years were fulfilled, *in the desert near Mount Sinai, an angel appeared to him in a flame blazing from a bush* that was on fire (Acts 7:30).

And here we pause, because we shall remain longer before this burning bush in the next meditation.

What characterizes this third period of Moses' life? I would call it the moment of discovery of the divine initiative in his life. Moses has arrived at the threshold of truth. I stress the word *discovery*, which is reminiscent of certain gospel words: to *discover* the treasure hidden in the field, a treasure which was there even if it was not seen; to *discover* the pearl of great price which unexpectedly appears among the others, and to discover it in one's own life, not in someone else's life. This treasure is right where I am, and I have lived many years without noticing it. This describes Moses' decisive moment.

Let us try to take a closer look at this moment, asking ourselves how the Lord gradually worked in Moses during these 40 years in the desert of Midian to prepare and dispose him for it. Since Moses has become more familiar to us, nearer to our experience, we can ask him what he did during those 40 years in the desert, how he passed his time, what he thought about during his sleepless nights, why he fled into the desert instead of taking up a business or travelling.

Gregory of Nyssa gives an answer to these questions. We know from the Bible (Ex 2:16-20) that when Moses arrives in the land of Midian, he meets the daughters of the priest Jethro and helps them—he is always the same generous Moses—and this priest with the keen eye appreciates him, gives him a new start and offers him one of his daughters as a wife. Gregory says: "Jethro let him choose the kind of life he wanted to live, and Moses chose solitude." Perhaps Gregory was speaking of himself, for after so many difficult experiences, he had acquired a lasting love of solitude.

I think that Moses himself would have answered our questions as follows: "What did I do for 40 years in the desert? I accepted the solitude; I even chose it." Moses did not fear the solitude.

When There Is a Void in Our Life

By way of digression, it is well-known that isolation and solitude differ. Isolation as such is something negative experienced by people who live desperately alone although they may be surrounded by others. They feel that they are misunderstood failures. Solitude, on the contrary, possesses a fundamental value for everyone, including modern men and women. There is a moment in which we come to realize that nothing has really satisfied us, that all our theories, all our experiences, all our hopes have brought us satisfaction only to a certain degree. There still remains a void that only God can fill. It is an experience that can be postponed as long as things are piled up, one overlapping the other, in the hope that one of them will fill the void. But when failure intervenes, we are able to enter that attitude of expectancy and vigilance which was Moses' state during these 40 years. It is a matter of learning to wait for God. "My efforts have not been successful, but the Lord will act!" Moses no longer places his hopes in himself and his own methods or in the capability of his people to respond. Perhaps at first Moses reviled them and persecuted them. But then he would have reflected and concluded: "We have all failed. I too have been at fault; I was too demanding. I left Pharaoh, but hoped at the same time to become a leader myself. It is not completely unjust that things turned out this way, because in the end I sought my own glory and wanted to make a monument to myself out of my people."

That is how Moses' solitude looks. He lets all his disappointment, pain and anger rise to the surface, without masking or suppressing anything, but facing it all, because he is not afraid to look into his life. It is a moment in which Moses finds himself in a situation similar to that of another great prophet, recorded in the First Book of Kings, the prophet who with him stands beside Jesus on the Mount of the Transfiguration — Elijah. In contrast to Moses, Elijah had enjoyed immense success.

On Mount Carmel he had overcome the prophets of Baal in a spectacular victory. He seemed to have arrived at the summit of his power. But immediately thereafter the Bible shows us how the great, courageous Elijah, who had challenged the 400 prophets of Baal, is frightened and escapes. He is afraid of being murdered and flees so fast that he leaves his servant behind and goes into the desert. After a day's journey he sits down under a furze bush and wishes he were dead. "Yahweh, I have had enough," he moans. "Take my life; I am no better than my ancestors" (1 Kgs 19:4). He had thought he was better than others, but then he realizes his mistake and gets rid of his bitterness. The same thing happens to Moses. Gradually, in the situation in which he finds himself, prayer emerges, that spirit of supplication which is found in Psalm 31; I would like to call it the prayer of Moses in the desert. Moses begins to understand that there has been a plan to his life, a plan that concerns not only himself but Yahweh as well. He had never realized that his work was the work of Yahweh; he had regarded it only as his work, until it fell apart in his hands. Now he is in prayer before Yahweh, humbly asking: "Lord, what does all this mean? Why did you let things come to this pass? If you will, please let me know."

In Which of These Periods Am I?

Now, at the conclusion of our meditation, I suggest we ask ourselves the question I proposed at the beginning: Where am I? In which period of Moses' life, in which of the 40-year spans, do I find myself? What is the characteristic element of my present experience? Is it joy, euphoria and enthusiasm? Or bitterness and failure? Or resignation—good resignation or the resignation born of helplessness?

What did Moses come to understand? I would say that he understood the divine initiative in his life; he understood that it is not he who was interested in God, but God who was interested in him. This is the fundamental principle of the good news of

25

the gospel. It is not we who have sought God, but God who seeks us. Consequently, it is not Moses who has compassion on the people, but God who has compassion and gives to Moses the gift of sharing in this compassion. This is really and truly a Pasch for Moses, and there will be others in his life. This is actually a radical passage from the time in which Moses seeks God to the time in which God seeks Moses. From this moment on, Moses' real mission can begin.

Moses and the Burning Bush

The texts for this meditation are Acts 7:30-31 and Exodus 3:1-10. Additional texts to keep in mind are Exodus 6:2-13 and 6:28—7:7, as well as two New Testament texts applicable to our theme, John 11:28 and Matthew 9:35—10:1. As prayer I would suggest Psalm 18, the psalm of the divine initiative.

Let us ask the Lord for the grace to enter into the scene of the burning bush in humility and truth. I propose to proceed by dealing with three very simple questions: 1) What does Moses do? 2) What does Moses hear? 3) What does Moses understand?

1. What Does Moses Do?

Moses Wonders

In this meditation let us keep Acts 7:30-31 and Exodus 3:1-3 side by side in our mind's eye. From Acts we learn that the first thing Moses does is wonder. While Moses is there in the desert, shepherding his father-in-law's flock, he sees at some distance a bush that is burning without being consumed. In Stephen's discourse he comments on this scene by saying, "Moses was amazed by what he saw" (Acts 7:31). I am very gratified to see that Moses, at 80 years of age, is able to wonder at something, to become interested in something new. Let us imagine ourselves in this great plain of Horeb at about 5,600 feet above sea level, with tall mountains towering all around in alternating terraces of sand and rock. On one of these terraces stands our bush. Think for a moment of what Moses could have done. He could have said to himself, "It's a fire. If it spreads it could be dangerous for the flock. I'd better go away and put the sheep at a distance." Or he could have thought, "This is something supernatural. It's better not to fall into a trap. I'll go and leave this to the younger generation if they are interested in it. They have more enthusiasm. I've already had my experiences, and they're enough for me."

Instead, Moses let himself be seized by the capacity, proper to children, of becoming interested in something new. We could think that this detail was just something added to the account. But I see in it a profound psychological insight on the part of Stephen, who intuitively understood that Moses, after having been in the desert for 40 years, worn out by failure but progressively purified by that state of vigilance and expectation on which we have already meditated, was now ripe for a new childhood, ripe to receive the newness of God. Perhaps Moses thought, "I'm a poor, frustrated man, but God can make something new out of me."

So Moses wonders, and then, the account in Acts continues, instead of not caring and going his way, *"he went nearer to look at it,"* as this passage (*proserkomenon de autou . . . katanoēsai*) is usually translated. But the Greek word *katanoēsai* means more than "to look at"; it really indicates the *nous*, the mind. As when Jesus tells us to "think of the ravens" (*katanoēsate tous korakos*) (Lk 12:24), it means to pay attention, consider, reflect, try to understand. Here the liberty of spirit that Moses has acquired in the process of purification is manifest. If he were still an embittered, resigned person, he would have been satisfied to say, "This is strange, but it doesn't concern me." But no, he wants to understand, to see what it is all about. He is a man very much alive, even in his old age.

Moses Is Curious

Now, continuing the story in Exodus, we read, "Moses said, 'I must go across and see this strange sight, and why the bush is not being burnt up' " (Ex 3:3). He is asking, "How can this be?" Moses is a man who lets questions arise within himself. He is no longer the person who already has everything systematized and catalogued, who has everything figured out. Now he is able to let himself be challenged by questions that require careful answering. "I must go across and see this strange sight." To "go across" is not exactly what is signified by the Hebrew word *sur*, which means "to make an excursion or a long tour." It gives the impression of an explicit resolution: I will understand. I think we could visualize the situation as follows. In the desert there are plateaus at different levels, and one must often make a long detour in order to reach a higher level. Moses happens to be at a lower level with his flock when he sees the bush on a higher plain and decides: "I'll go up. I'll make the detour. I want to see what this is." It means leaving the flock, perhaps in danger, and going out into the heat of the sun. Consequently we sense Moses' attitude in these words: "I must go across and see this strange sight — and why the bush is not being burnt up." It is as though he is saying to himself: "Although I am a poor man and a failure, God can do something new with me. I want to get interested in this, to comprehend and get to the bottom of it, to know why." Notice here that the big question Moses had been asking himself for 40 years returns: "Why did God permit that failure? If he loves his people, why didn't he use me to save them? Why didn't he seize the opportunity I gave him?" This why that Moses had cultivated, refined and purified emerges again at the sight of this unexpected vision. But by now Moses has grown and taken on the characteristics of a profound, mature, purified person, open to what is new.

Taking this episode of Moses as point of departure, we can reflect at depth on the attitude of a person before the mystery of

God. Such a person could say, "I am not interested." On the other hand, he or she could respond with, "I want to perceive, to be able to explain it, to know." This is a matter of the primary movement of the human soul, that unconditional desire to know and to understand which, as is rightfully said, stands at the origin of everything human in the world. For if in this world there is anything beyond the animal, beyond mere eating, drinking and reproducing, if there is anything human, if — as Paul says in the Letter to the Philippians — there are affections, relations of friendship and mutual understanding, it all springs from this very simple affirmation: "I want to understand." Human civilization itself is built upon this foundation.

Moses, therefore, is a man brought back to the primary root of his humanity and placed before the mystery of God. He responds with that unreserved desire to know from which everything human originates. Because Moses wants to know, he is now ready to exert himself. He abandons the comfort of the plain, in which he can sit in the shadow of his tent, and begins the wearisome ascent up the mountain. He likewise leaves the flock, solely in order to finally arrive at knowing. This "knowing" of Moses is something that burns within him; it is a passion that has not abated. Purification has rendered it simpler and freer. Moses does not ascend the mountain in order to seek a new personal success. He goes because he wants to know things as they really are; he wants to face the truth as it is.

Comments Based on the Rabbinic Literature

Two rabbinic texts could be cited here in connection with our subject. The first is a passage that speaks of the paschal *Haggadah*, the rite according to which the Hebrew Pasch is celebrated. Some youths are listening to the account of the Paschal Night. One falls asleep, while another queries, "What does this story of Egypt have to do with me?" But a third really wants to know: "Why are we celebrating this feast? What meaning does it have for us?" This is the attitude of Moses as he poses that basic question, "How can this be?"

The second rabbinic text is a very beautiful account of Rabbi Akiba. Shortly after Jesus' time, around the year 135, he was martyred by the Romans. He is a key figure in the development of Judaism after Jesus. Here I shall give a synopsis of his history. Rabbi Akiba was very poor, having led a life of privation for 40 years. At the age of 40, as he stood one day before a fountain flowing with water, he noticed that the stone under the fountain was hollowed out. On asking who had hollowed it out he was told, "The water that falls on it day by day. Do you not recall the words in Job (14:19) according to which water wears away stone?" Rabbi Akiba then thought to himself, "If water, which is so soft, hollows out rock, which is so hard, could not the words of the Torah, which are as hard as rock, hollow out my heart, which is the softness of flesh?" So it came about that at 40 he began to study the Torah. Together with his son, he went to a teacher with his request, "Master, teach me the Torah." Painstakingly, letter by letter, he gradually learned Leviticus and the entire Torah. After having mastered it, he appeared before Rabbi Eliezer and Rabbi Joshua with the petition, "My teachers, reveal to me the meaning of the Mishnah" (a collection of writings that preserve the oral tradition as a commentary on the Torah). The masters began to expound the Mishnah by reading a *Halakah* to him (a passage containing a moral prescription that explains a part of the Pentateuch). When Rabbi Akiba had heard the *Halakah*, he went out for a walk and asked himself, "Why was this letter *aleph* written? Why was this *beth* written? Why was this thing said?" He went back and asked his teachers, but they could not answer him.

Note that in this anecdote we have a parallel to the scene of the boy Jesus with the teachers of the law. Most likely Jesus asked very simple questions and precisely in this way silenced the great teachers. Jesus, and Rabbi Akiba after him, had the courage to pose essential questions, questions that are never asked because they seem so obvious, but from which everything else proceeds.

2. What Does Moses Hear?

Since the text of Acts gives only a summary account, we shall now turn to Exodus: "When Yahweh saw him going across to look, God called to him from the middle of the bush. 'Moses, Moses!' he said" (Ex 3:4). Moses hears his name.

Imagine the shock, the fear mingled with amazement, that Moses experiences on hearing his name called in the desert, a place in which no one was living. Moses becomes aware that someone who knows him must be there, someone who is interested in him. He had considered himself rejected, unsuccessful, abandoned. Regardless of that, someone is calling his name in the middle of the desert. It is a startling experience, and perhaps one we too have undergone somewhere — maybe in a large city — in which we thought no one knew us but all of a sudden we heard someone calling us by name. Now Moses hears his name called twice: "Moses, Moses."

What does this double call mean? For me, it evokes the following reflection. In the Bible it is rather rare for a person to be called twice, but there are a few instances. The first, in Genesis 22:1, marks the highpoint in Abraham's life when he was summoned to sacrifice his son. It was the moment in which the sincerity of his way of life up to that time was to be tested. Hence, the double mention of his name: "Abraham, Abraham." Another passage that I would mention is the one in the First Book of Samuel in which he is called during the night: "Samuel, Samuel" (1 Sm 3:10). Here too we are at a turning point in Israel's history. The confusing period of the Judges is ending and the time of the kings, which will occasion a new nearness of God to his people, is beginning. We could also cite Luke 22:31: "Simon, Simon! Look, Satan has got his wish to sift you all like wheat." This instance likewise represents a climax in Peter's life. There is still another text that seems to me to be important: "Martha, Martha" (Lk 10:41). This episode, simple enough in itself, concerning a household matter, is nevertheless very important to Luke because it is the counterpart to the story of the Good Samaritan. Mary represents those who listen to God's word. Martha, on the other hand, is the person filled with good will who dedicates herself to works of charity — as Moses did in the first period of his life — and throws herself so much into her activity that priorities become confused. This passage is truly important in that it shows us how Martha, seized with the urge to do something good, indeed very good — to prepare a fine dinner for Jesus — has at a certain point reversed all her values. While Jesus has come to her house as teacher, it is Martha who turns teacher and wants to instruct Jesus about what he should say and do, thus completely inverting the sense of the gospel. Basically this is the same mistake that Moses made at first in thinking he had the situation fully in hand and could tell God what to do. Of course Moses did not know about Simon or Martha, but he was familiar with the traditions regarding Abraham and therefore could be aware of the significance of this double call.

God Takes the Initiative

It seems to me that all the facts recorded in the Bible are decisive in nature. So it is that Moses has arrived at a decisive moment in his life, a point where he has to be truly available and not relapse into past mistakes. This fills him with fear: "What is going to happen to me now?" Presently he hears something that he was perhaps not expecting. He who had dashed forward with all his might to see the burning bush would have been gratified to hear himself praised for coming and for not letting the bitterness of the past win the upper hand over him. Instead he hears a voice saying to him, "Come no nearer. . . . Take off your sandals, for the place where you are standing is holy ground" (Ex 3:5). Here the words of Jesus to Mary of Magdala come to

33

mind: "Do not cling to me" (Jn 20:17). Mary approaches Jesus with love but still encapsulating him in her passé view of things, whereas she should change her attitude.

When we let ourselves be carried away with the desire to investigate something, we believe that we already possess what we are seeking, and in a certain sense we do possess it in perceiving it. In this way we end up by inserting the religious phenomena that we experience, including the divine activity, into our own mental framework. This process is inevitable, for it is a fact that we cannot understand things without starting from an intellectual framework that we already possess and referring them to it. That is what Moses was ardently trying to do — to consider this phenomenon of the burning bush as a part of his view of God, of history and of God's presence in history. Then God says to him: "Moses, that doesn't go! Take your sandals off, because you are not going to come to me by enclosing me in your own ideas. You are not the one to integrate me into your personal synthesis. Instead, I want to fit you into my plan."

This is the meaning of removing one's sandals and approaching haltingly, as one would do when walking barefoot over stones, uncertain with the uncertainty of a person who is wondering what is going to happen next. The fact is that no one can march triumphantly into availability to the mystery of God. The Moslems still have the custom of removing their footwear on entering the mosque, as though to step before God on tiptoe, in silence, not imposing their own pace on God but letting themselves be absorbed and integrated into God's pace.

So Moses hears: "Come no nearer. . . . Take off your sandals, for the place where you are standing is holy ground." Imagine Moses' confusion on hearing these words. Is this holy ground? This cursed desert, the abode of jackals, of desolation and aridity, where only bandits roam and no one would want to settle for good? This desert where I felt so lonely, wretched and frustrated — is this holy ground? Is this God's presence? Is this the place where God reveals himself?

34

3. What Does Moses Understand?

At this point Moses understands what the divine initiative is. It is not he who is seeking God and therefore has to go to purified and holy places in order to find him. Rather, it is God who seeks Moses and seeks him where he is, in the place where he happens to be, wherever that is, even if it is a miserable, abandoned, accursed place devoid of resources. Several passages in the Bible speak of the desolation characteristic of the desert, the haunt of wild dogs, snakes and scorpions. And precisely this is holy ground. Here God is present and here he reveals his glory.

We could pause a moment to contemplate how Moses experienced his own change of horizon, his true conversion, his new manner of recognizing God. Until now God was for Moses someone for whom he had to *do* much: to start a revolution, sacrifice his own privileged position, rush to his people and spend himself for them only to be scorned and rejected by them in the end. Now he finally begins to realize that God is different. Up to this point he has thought of God as one who exploited him for a while and then deserted him, a master more exacting than all others, more demanding than Pharaoh even. Now he starts to understand that God is merciful and loving, is concerned about him, the worst of failures, forgotten by his people.

In order to help us better understand this intuition of Moses, I would like to cite John 11:28 where Mary of Bethany is mourning her brother. She is weeping so bitterly that she remains at home. For her, everything is lost. Surely she is a woman of faith and believes that her brother will rise again, but humanly speaking she is desperate, incapable of being comforted by any word. Now all the joy of family life is at an end. The account continues: "She [Martha] went and called her sister Mary, saying in a low voice, 'The Master is here and wants to see you.' " Just picture Mary's surprise. She had felt forsaken, hopeless, disconsolate, and suddenly she is told that right there close by, beside the tomb of her desperation, the Master is calling her by name

35

and has a word for her. Such an experience awakens the awareness of the divine initiative in one's own life.

Returning to Moses, we find him listening as God says, "I am the God of your ancestors . . . the God of Abraham, the God of Isaac and the God of Jacob" (Ex 3:6). Note how interesting these words are and how they cause Moses' dismayed soul to regain its balance. Moses is now aware that he has not understood anything about God; at all events, he thinks that this is a new and different God. But actually God is saying to him: "I am the God of your ancestors. If you had understood more, you would have recognized that I am the same God that Abraham, Isaac and Jacob knew. I dealt with them in the same way I am dealing with you." The Lord had always been a God who was concerned about the abandoned and those who felt hopeless and ruined. This reassuring speech is beautiful because a person like Moses, who has bungled everything, runs the risk of forgetting, but then the Lord recalls for him the entire past that must be remembered and reflected on so that God's initiative may become manifest.

We may never forget that our God is the same God of those who have educated us in the faith, the God of our parents, who taught us to pray, the God of those who formed us spiritually and of all those who have preceded us on the way of the gospel. However we may have manipulated this God of ours for our own purposes, there is a moment in which we are finally called — before the burning bush — to truly understand who he is.

The God of Mercy

In order to understand how this God really is, we shall now continue with our text from Exodus:

> Yahweh then said, "I have indeed seen the misery of my people in Egypt. I have heard them crying for help on account of their taskmasters. Yes, I am well aware of their sufferings. And I have come down to rescue them from the clutches of the Egyptians and bring them up out of that country, to a country rich and broad, to a country flowing

with milk and honey. . . . Yes indeed, the Israelites' cry
for help has reached me, and I have also seen the cruel
way in which the Egyptians are oppressing them" (Ex 3:7-
9).

Notice how carefully worded the text is, all in the first person:
"I have seen," "I have heard," "I am well aware," "I have come
down," and so on. Note also that Moses is being implicitly re-
proached: "You, Moses, thought you were a very cultivated person, well versed in the knowledge of human nature. You thought
you understood your people and their misery. You believed that
it was up to you to take the initiative in understanding them and
then to entreat me so that I might understand them too. However, it was I who first understood them; it is I who understand
all these things, I who see and hear. You, Moses, thought that
you were the first to have discovered the beauty of freedom, de-
sirous as you were to have others taste it also, but you did not
succeed. Nevertheless, all that was my doing. You never thought
that it was my work; instead you threw yourself desperately into
it, thinking it was your work and that everything depended on
you. Now you are coming to realize that I see, I hear . . . and
what is more, if you find in yourself any compassion for the
people, it comes from me. If you have any sense of freedom, it
is I who give it to you. If there is any intellectual curiosity in
you, it is mine."

One final aspect still emerges from the patristic literature,
which comments on our text in the light of the New Testament.
" 'I have come down' says the Lord" (Ex 3:8): It is Jesus who
has come down in order to say, "I have seen and heard the misery of my people. From nearby, I know it, and their cry has
reached my ears."

What happens at this point? God says, "Now, go!" See how
God's pedagogy operates! Once Moses is freed from the bonds
of his own presumption about saving the Israelites and has been
rendered responsive to the reality of things, God sends him
again, as though nothing had happened, as though he had never

failed. God reinstates him and shows full confidence in him: "I am sending you to Pharaoh." Moses feels completely taken into God's hands and sent anew, not to accomplish a work of his own but God's work.

Moses Is Commissioned for God's Work

In order to shed still more light on our subject, I recommend another beautiful text on which it would be worthwhile to meditate at length, the passage that describes the compassion of Jesus, the Good Shepherd (Mt 9:35—10:1). The account, found at the conclusion of the first part of the gospel according to Matthew, presents Jesus — like Moses — as mighty in word (the Sermon on the Mount, chapters 5-7) and in deed (the ten miracles, chapters 8-9). I shall now single out some points for reflection.

"Jesus made a tour through all the towns and villages, teaching in their synagogues, proclaiming the good news of the kingdom and curing all kinds of disease and all kinds of illness" (Mt 9:35). This means that Jesus was mighty in deed and word among the people. "And when he saw the crowds he felt sorry for them because they were harassed and dejected, like sheep without a shepherd. Then he said to his disciples . . ." Here we would have expected Jesus to tell the disciples, "Go!" Instead, he says, "Pray!" "Ask the Lord of the harvest to send out labourers to his harvest" (Mt 9:36-37). This hopeful instruction is very important. Jesus is trying to say: "Do not think you have to throw yourself into the work as though it were yours. The work belongs to the Lord of the harvest, the Father. Do not presume to fling yourself into it as Moses did in the beginning, but let yourself be sent by God." "Ask the Lord to send out labourers" does not mean to pray, "Lord, send someone," but rather, "Make me worthy of being sent so that I may approach this work not because it pleases me and is what I have programmed for myself, but because it is the work that you are giving me." And, in fact, immediately afterward the text reads:

"He summoned the twelve disciples and gave them authority over unclean spirits with power to drive them out and to cure all kinds of disease and all kinds of illness" (Mt 10:1). Then, after the names of the twelve apostles are cited, Jesus commissions them: "And as you go, proclaim that the kingdom of Heaven is close at hand. Cure the sick, raise the dead, cleanse those suffering from virulent skin-diseases, drive out devils. You received without charge, give without charge" (Mt 10:7-8). Jesus is saying: "I transmit to you my work, my apostolic compassion; that is, I transfer to you my ability to understand people. Now, using this ability, go and preach the kingdom, cure the sick, and do everything without charge."

The parallel to the story of Moses is evident. Moses too will be accepted for God's work only after having been purified and renewed interiorly by letting himself be educated to missionary compassion.

Third Meditation

Moses, Pharaoh and Ourselves

This meditation is an attempt to comment on the narrative of the plagues in Egypt as recorded in Exodus 5-11. I recommend a calm reading of these chapters. (You may omit chapter 6, a second account of the call of Moses, on which we have already reflected.) As we reflect on the proposed theme, we intend to arouse in ourselves a spirit of penance, not in the sense that we want to be occupied with recognizing the sin in ourselves in a sadistic way. Rather, we aim to obtain an idea of how abundant God's grace is and to place ourselves sincerely before the superabundant fullness of God's mercy, that is, of the gospel, keeping in mind that "however much sin increased, grace was always greater" (Rom 5:20). A meditation on the episode following the call of Moses — his mission to Pharaoh and the plagues of Egypt — seems eminently suited for this purpose.

How Is This Meditation Made?

The account is quite lengthy, covering more than five chapters. We could examine it exegetically, isolating the various traditions that have come together in a kind of epic flow, like a great poem. At times the narrative gives the impression of being like a symphony in 10 parts, in which some themes are introduced, then repeated and developed. It all serves, however, as a commentary on God's words: "I will lead you out with strong arm." Among the many aspects of this account that could be considered, I shall limit myself to proposing only one: human relations. In other words we need not pause to define the exact nature and meaning of the various plagues — the flies, the red colored water of the Nile, the ulcers, the locusts, and so on. Rather, we shall attend to the persons in the scene and to the relationship among them; as St. Ignatius recommends we shall "consider the persons." In our text, there are two principal persons, corresponding to our first two meditation points: 1) Who is Pharaoh and what does he do? and 2) Who is Moses and what does he do? We intend therefore to ascertain how much of Pharaoh there is *in us* and how much of Moses there is *in us*, and to examine how the relationship between Moses and Pharaoh concerns us and our paschal experience of passing from death to life, from an inauthentic life to the authentic life of the gospel.

As a kind of appendix I shall add a third point regarding the obstinacy of Pharaoh, a constantly recurring theme in these chapters: "Pharaoh was stubborn."

1. Who is the Pharaoh in Us?

Who is Pharaoh? From the biblical texts I gather two traits characteristic of him. First of all he is an outstanding gentleman, intelligent, shrewd, capable, even democratic, if you wish. In short, he is an attractive person. Let me explain. Moses and Aaron go to him and announce the plagues of flies, locusts, and so forth. He listens to them, discusses with them and enters into a dialogue with them. He is, therefore, a man who knows the rules of democracy, of fair play. His liberty of spirit is quite extraordinary. Take, for example, the episode in which Moses and Aaron approach him for the first time and proclaim:

> "This is what Yahweh, God of Israel, says, 'Let my people go, so that they can hold a feast in my honour in the desert.' " "Who is Yahweh," Pharaoh replied, "for me to obey what he says and let Israel go?" (Ex 5:1-2).

Basically, Pharaoh has a right to his point of view: "You talk to me about Yahweh. This is your religion, but you may not impose on me a religion that is not mine. I have my own principles."

Then after the plague of flies, Pharaoh calls Moses and Aaron and says, "Go and sacrifice to your God, inside the country" (Ex 8:21). This signifies that he tries to negotiate and arrive at an agreement.

> "That would never do," Moses said, "since what we sacrifice to Yahweh our God is outrageous to the Egyptians. If the Egyptians see us offering sacrifices which outrage them, won't they stone us? We shall make a three-days' journey into the desert to sacrifice to Yahweh our God, as he has ordered us." Pharaoh said, "I will let you go and sacrifice to Yahweh your God in the desert, provided you do not go very far. Pray for me" (Ex 8:22-24).

What skill in bargaining! First he says, "Offer sacrifice here." Then, "Sacrifice in the desert, but not too far away — a three days' distance is too much — and pray for me."

A Person Who Wants to Be Fair

After the eighth plague, that of the locusts, we witness another attempt at negotiation.

> So Moses and Aaron were brought back to Pharaoh who said to them, "Go and worship Yahweh your God. But who are to go?" Moses replied, "We shall take our young men and our old men, we shall take our sons and daughters, our flocks and our herds, since we are going to hold a feast in Yahweh's honour." Pharaoh said, "So I must let you go with your wives and children! May Yahweh preserve you!" (Ex 10:8-10).

But then follows: "Plainly, you are up to no good!" Pharaoh, being a very keen and intelligent man, realizes that although Moses and Aaron speak of three days, in reality they intend to leave for good. Hence he attempts to negotiate again: "Oh, no!

You men may go and worship Yahweh since that was your original request" (Ex 10:11).

Later, after the ninth plague, there is another instance of bargaining: "Pharaoh summoned Moses and said, 'Go and worship Yahweh, but your flocks and herds are to stay here. Your wives and children can go with you too' " (Ex 10:24).

Pharaoh not only negotiates skillfully, tries to strike a compromise and understands the situation of others, but he also is willing to re-evaluate his thinking in the face of new developments. Whereas at first he had declared, "I know nothing of Yahweh," after the plague of horseflies he asks Moses, "Pray for me." He begins to recognize in what is happening something important that he could not see in the beginning. And he appears capable of acknowledging his faults. After the plague of hail, Pharaoh confesses:

> "This time, I have sinned. Yahweh is in the right; I and my subjects are in the wrong. Pray to Yahweh, for we cannot bear any more of this thunder and hail. I promise to let you go. You need stay no longer" (Ex 9:27-28).

This man really seems to have arrived at repentance.

Pharaoh's discourse after the plague of locusts is even more explicit:

> Pharaoh sent urgently for Moses and Aaron and said, "I have sinned against Yahweh your God and against you. Now forgive my sin, I implore you, just this once, and entreat Yahweh your God to turn this deadly thing away from me" (Ex 10:16).

These very beautiful words will be echoed by the Prodigal Son: "Father, I have sinned against heaven and against you."

But He Encounters Certain Difficulties

Pharaoh therefore is intelligent, sagacious and capable of submitting to evidence. But he is at the same time conditioned by his position, his privileges, his status as Pharaoh. Herein lies his real dilemma. Pharaoh would like to let the Israelites go, but he cannot because he would be acting against too many personal interests. We can see this, for instance, in his first dramatic instructions to the overseers of forced labor:

> "You are lazy, lazy," he retorted. "That is why you say, 'Let us go and sacrifice to Yahweh.' Get back to your work at once" (Ex 5:17-18).

In short, Pharaoh realizes that if this plan succeeds, Egypt's economy will suffer and workers will be lacking. But work and productivity are necessary to ensure the empire's grandeur.

Imagine Pharaoh during a discussion with Aaron and Moses. He invites them to be seated and says: "Look, what you propose to do is insane. To go out into the desert to die like rats is not in your own interests. Besides, you would leave Egypt in a disastrous situation. In my position of responsibility I cannot permit such chaos. Egypt has an orderly structure, which I am obliged to maintain. Last but not least, if you remain here you will have bread, work and security." This poor man comes to the verge of recognizing his sin, but then he retracts everything and withdraws. If this foolish people that wants to go out to the desert actually dies of hunger and thirst, then it means death for the Egyptians too. There will be starvation, hard times and disaster. Pharaoh regards his action as a matter of duty, office and responsibility. Such is Pharaoh: intelligent, perspicacious, skilled, noble, but bound by his privileges, his position and his social status.

Here let us consider who the Pharaoh in ourselves is, what he represents. The figure of Pharaoh sums up all the circumstances that condition us. Without them we would conduct ourselves differently, but they draw us into their vortex. Our personal conditionings are legion, and psychoanalysis helps us to discover them. They surround us, always ready to spring into action. Perhaps, unaware of them, we go on tranquilly, and then when certain occasions arise, a certain conditioning is triggered and makes us say and do things that we had never thought we would say or do.

The Power of Our Conditionings

It sometimes happens that people proclaim high principles in public, but when confronted with the least decision they withdraw: Not that! Pharaoh too tells himself, "In principle I am doing right. I cannot do differently. I am a man of integrity." The fact is that we are influenced by blind spots, that is, shadowy areas in which we do not see things at all. These are real blockages, often unconscious, but perhaps easily recognizable to others.

In addition there are group conditionings that involve us, that keep us captive inwardly and make us judge everything on the basis of common prejudices according to verbal ideologies and opinions already formed. This is particularly manifest when we say, "This is evident. It is not up for discussion." Even the tone of voice reveals that it is a statement conditioned by fear of facing the issue in earnest. For instance, a person could say, "No, there is a limit beyond which I cannot risk my dignity!" Nice words, beneath which we often hide everything that we do not want to place under discussion. My dignity? Which dignity? That of the privileged, of the well-off, of the church member, or that of the follower of Christ crucified?

These are our conditionings! It is useless to attempt to examine them by introspection; we will not see them. Only concrete occasions will reveal them to us, allowing those shadowy areas to appear.

Deficient Charity

Here I would like to cite a rather strong statement of St. Augustine. It is a dramatic affirmation of human powerlessness in the face of those situations in which love is challenged to prove itself. Hence St. Augustine says that we can speak of sin — not in a purely moral sense, of course, but in the more general sense — whenever we fail to respond to the values that the love of God proposes to us, "whenever the love that should be present [in certain situations that always involve an encounter with another person] is not there, or when love is less than it ought to be, whether this can be avoided or not."

For the most part, we know how to recognize all this in others, but not in ourselves. Sometimes, however, the Lord lets us sense that we too have our limitations. This happens above all in interpersonal relations when we are in a position to pardon sincerely, to accept someone who has criticized us or undermined our efforts or betrayed us. Then the obstacles in us surface.

Power wants power; Pharaoh is Pharaoh. He cannot be asked to humble himself because as Pharaoh he instinctively retains possession of his own privileges and cannot surrender them. This is precisely the drama of human existence, of individuals and above all of groups — group privileges, group power in the world, in nations, in the church, in religious institutions, in religious houses. It is the power of Pharaoh; it penetrates into everything and is present with its tentacles everywhere, in all of us. On the surface this power, as we have said, is not ugly; on the contrary it appears noble and courteous and speaks very prudently. But the limits assert themselves: "No, that may not be done." That is Pharaoh.

If we would like to know still more about the Pharaoh in us, we can meditate on the list of 12 ways in which Pharaoh works as given in Mark 7:22, which begins, "For it is from within, from the human heart, that evil intentions emerge." The Pharaoh in us is this wickedness of intention that does not come from without but rather originates within us and is then able to harden in the groups and in the various forms of resistance and power disseminated everywhere. These are pharaonic activities of possessiveness and exploitation of others: "Fornication, theft, murder, adultery, avarice, malice, deceit, indecency, envy, slander, pride, folly." Each of these words expresses an attitude that resides in the heart not only of *some* men and women but of

47

every one of us. We possess within us all these tendencies to overpower, to possess and to appropriate others, if only with a little word of envy or a little gossip, which allows us to avenge the little power that the other has acquired. There we see Pharaoh already growing in ourselves.

2. Who Is Moses In Us?

If this is Pharaoh, who is Moses in us? The Moses in ourselves is above all the thrust of our freedom and of our desire to comprehend things as they are, to conform to them and to make decisions in keeping with them. It is expressed in Moses' question: "Why is the bush burning without being consumed? I will go and see." Moses within us is the desire to get to the bottom of everything and to question it. This drive is a small but dangerous instrument because it sets so many other impulses in motion; nevertheless, it is the only thing we possess that is really human and is profoundly ours. It is that gift which scripture calls *pneuma*, the human spirit, the capacity to face things and ask: "Why do I act — or react — that way?"

Then there is *Pneuma* with a capital P, the Spirit of God, the incessant effort with which God does everything in order to free and inspire whatever actual possibilities are present in our desire for authenticity, in our pneuma, which is imprisoned by conditionings of every kind. For anything can become an occasion for pharisaism if we adhere to it not as a gift of God but as our own possession. In that case we do not want the Lord, much less others, to question us. Moses represents God's effort to liberate us by bringing our authenticity into play, by repeatedly casting us into the boiling cauldron of the Spirit that loosens our rigidity and shakes our conditioning, enabling us to approach everything anew with a pliable and free spirit.

I am not recommending an attitude that is disposed to agree to everything without question, but rather one that, when confronted with a situation, appraises its good and bad aspects, ready either to accept or refuse it, after having prayed, listened and reflected in order to be certain that it is the Spirit that is moving us. Moses knows what he wants; in his encounters with Pharaoh he can wait, hesitate, be patient, insist and say no, because he has within him the Spirit which is such a pliant, adaptable, flexible and at the same time incomparably tenacious strength. This is Moses in ourselves.

Moses Works With Words. . .

Thus far, we have seen that Pharaoh is fundamentally a man who is constrained by his conditioning. He squarely refuses to accede to the requests of the Hebrews, although he tries to hide behind the appearances of listening and dialogue and even behind gestures of a religious nature such as repentance and the plea for mercy. In contrast, how is God's liberating power expressed in Moses? And how is this liberating strength of God manifested in us?

First of all, let us examine how this power is not expressed. It is not demonstrated in violence, as in the case of the early Moses, who aspired to save his people in a violent way. The later Moses, on the contrary, is a person who talks, and in such a way that he tries to persuade. The first Moses did not even say a word but immediately attacked the Egyptian and killed him. Now we have before us the Moses of the word, the word of God: "Yahweh said to Moses . . . 'You will then *say* to Pharaoh . . . ' " (Ex 4:19,22). And observe the indefatigable insistence — almost paradoxical to us — with which, before a Pharaoh who does not want to understand, the Lord repeats to Moses, "Go to Pharaoh and say to him . . . ." This is the untiring strength of the word of God that is continually repeating: "Free yourself, become authentic, listen to me!"

If in the beginning we noticed Pharaoh's liberality in not imprisoning Moses or having him executed, here we can see the courage with which Moses returns to Pharaoh, even if Pharaoh is increasingly enraged and upset. Moses believes in the power of the word, even though he knows that Pharaoh is obstinate. It is obstinacy that is foreseen, but even in such a case God works through his persuasive word. Therefore he says to Moses, "Go to Pharaoh and say to him . . . " as though Moses would be able to convince him. This, then, is a primary characteristic of the God who liberates, that he uses the word and persuasion even when the circumstances are not promising.

. . . And With Signs

Besides the word, right from the beginning of the narrative we find signs also. At first they are harmless, almost humorous: Aaron casts his staff down before Pharaoh and his servants, and it becomes a serpent. Then Pharaoh summons his wizards and they repeat the trick. The sign is offered in the first place as a simple sign. But Pharaoh, not wanting to lose the privilege of his power, attempts to produce similar signs in order to convince himself that he is not dealing with a real sign and can therefore rest assured. God, however, speaks in signs that gradually become really tormenting, increasingly hard and troublesome. These plagues — flies, unpotable water, and so forth — represent the malaise of the inauthentic person. On the basis of our experience we can say that God does not punish for the love of it, but human beings — Pharaoh and all the people of Egypt representing those who refuse to accept the liberating word of God — become more and more entangled in their own difficulties and conditionings. Actually, every time we have not listened to the word of the Lord that requires us to be more true, more authentic, more responsive to love and readier to offer service than to claim it, we have felt within us the signs of inner imbalance. These are the manifestations of the little slaveries and conditionings to which we surrender. They are all those forms of malaise that undermine us interiorly: fear of facing certain situations, certain kinds of painful and prolonged fatigue, certain forms of ill humor, a certain inability to pray, in short, not knowing how to be happy. Whenever we are not completely happy, it means that there is something, some conditioning hindering us, even though we may not speak about it or admit it.

What is the fundamental evil to which all others can be reduced? It is the inability to love and to effectively practice love of God and especially love of neighbor. To love God can be easy. Love of neighbor, however, is difficult and consists in responding to the actual situation of our neighbor's need, even where the person does not deserve our help, is not worthy of it. If we are not equal to this situation, the result is dissatisfaction, uneasiness and disgust, which involve the person and community, groups and institutions. This is the punishment of Egypt.

Regarding this subject we can also add that there is such a thing as a definitive hardening. At a certain point Pharaoh closes himself off; he remains Pharaoh because he wants to. He intends to retain his privileges, without putting anything up for discussion, and so he is swallowed up by the sea. We know, and the church teaches, that the moment can come in which we remain obdurate in our inability to really love. After having repeatedly refused, we are left as though trapped in this incapacity, in this definitive hardening. That is what we call punishment par excellence, one that proceeds first of all from ourselves. We have closed ourselves to the words, signs and chastisements that the Lord in his mercy has permitted.

3. Pharaoh's Heart Hardens

The texts that mention this theme are numerous enough (Ex 4:21; 7:3,14,22; 8:11,15,28; et al.). To these may be added the passage in the Letter to the Romans where St. Paul treats of God's hardening the heart of whomever he wills and investigates how this accords with human freedom (Rom 9). These are problems that I do not intend to discuss here. Instead, we can ask ourselves what we have experienced of Pharaoh's hardening of heart in ourselves.

First of all, let us inquire as to the nature of this hardening. It consists in the fact that Pharaoh recognizes that it would be advisable to yield — he even perseveres for a long time in the tendency to give in — but he cannot, because then he would cease to be Pharaoh and he does not want that. His hardening therefore represents emblematically that power which insists upon preserving itself and resists any transformations whatever.

Hardening Out of Obstinacy

Now if we apply this hardening to ourselves. I believe we can distinguish two basic accepted meanings of the term, two ways of interpreting it. In the first place, there is a hardening out of obstinacy. It is the more typical form, and comprises not only the hardening of atheists who do not want to believe or of sensual sinners who refuse to relinquish their vices — and hardly can, since they are so entrenched in them — but also includes an obstinacy that is manifested in religious and ecclesiastical sectors by those who believe themselves to be depositories of the truth in a possessive way. In that case the truth is no longer regarded as having been received from the church but is identified with their own history and their own person. Any attack on what is held to be the truth is regarded as a personal offense instead of an injustice to the church. In this way individuals are led to identify their personal history and personal identity with that which cannot but be true. And then they become hardened; they refuse to listen to reason. Some feel all the more bound to act this way if they happen to hold responsible positions in civil, social or ecclesial circles, positions that they have to defend. Such is the hardening of the heart out of obstinacy.

Hardening Out of Frailty

There is a second way of understanding the hardening of Pharaoh's heart, one that I call a hardening out of frailty.

We experience it on becoming aware that there are limits to our capacity to love. As long as circumstances are favorable, we do not notice it. When, however, the situation becomes more difficult, when we encounter life as a conflict of powers, opinions and interests, then we experience more acutely our practical inability to free ourselves and to love genuinely. It is then that the gospel description of the pagans is verified in us: We too greet those who greet us; we lend to those from whom we hope to receive back; we smile at those who smile at us and at those whom we fear, trying at the same time to keep them at a distance so that our integrity may not be endangered. Like Pharaoh, we too are afraid to love; we would rather negotiate and come to terms. Essentially, we are afraid to lose our life, and since Jesus says that anyone who does not lose his own life cannot be his disciple, we ought to realize that in this regard we are not his disciples. In this connection it is worthwhile recalling again the conditionings to which we are subject simply by the fact of being members of a group, a class, a society. A similar phenomenon can be noticed among peoples with very strong traditions. We Westerners, despite so much confusion, have the advantage of being able to do quite a few things independently. In some other social groups or nations, certain persons may not do certain things because the social group does not tolerate it, and this constitutes an absolute limit.

Realities of this kind recall for us the dramatic element in human existence of which the Letter to the Romans speaks: "The good thing I want to do, I never do; the evil thing which I do not want — that is what I do" (7:19). Concretely accepting these limitations, we easily arrive at reliving the parable of the barren fig tree. We would like to produce much fruit, and with God's grace we do succeed in some areas, but in others we are just not able to. The Lord makes us experience the limits of our pharaonic existence and lets us come to the point of not knowing which way to turn so that we might call on his saving help and realize the incredible superabundance of his mercy.

Fourth Meditation

The Passage Through the Sea of Reeds

The basic text for this meditation is Exodus 14:5—15:20. In addition we shall use two other texts as supplements: 1 Corinthians 10:1-2 and Matthew 8:19-20. In the *Spiritual Exercises* of St. Ignatius, this meditation on the passage through the Sea of Reeds would correspond to the meditation on the kingdom (*Spiritual Exercises*, 91-100) and its dynamic of self-offering: Where is the Lord leading me? Let us courageously offer ourselves to follow his initiative!

The Central Event of Our Faith

We are meditating, then, on the passage through the Sea of Reeds. Our text from Exodus is a fundamental one, the paschal text par excellence. In our present Easter liturgy the third reading of the Easter Vigil (Ex 14:15—15:1) constitutes a central element, followed by the canticle of Exodus 15:1-7,17-18. If we were to look merely at the words, we might think that Exodus 12 should be the principal Easter text, since it contains the description of the Passover feast: "This month must be the first of all the months for you, the first month of your year" (Ex 12:2). Nevertheless, although the word *Passover* should refer primarily to the feast of unleavened bread and to the night in which the lamb was eaten — which is indeed treated in Exodus 12 — Christian tradition has extended the meaning of the word *Passover* to include the passage through the Sea of Reeds, which even eventually assumed the typological role that assimilated all the rest. The Fathers of the church have amply commented on the passage through the sea, interpreting it as the Christian Pasch, as the baptism that signifies our dedication to Christ.

This event is likewise mentioned in the *Exsultet*. I have in mind the Easter Vigil, on which everything else in Christian life depends. In the *Exsultet* we hear:

> This is the night when first you saved our fathers:
>> you freed the people of Israel from their slavery
>> and led them dry-shod through the sea.
>
> This is the night when the pillar of fire
>> destroyed the darkness of sin!
>
> This is the night when Christians everywhere,
>> washed clean of sin
>> and freed from all defilement,
>> are restored to grace and grow together in holiness.

This already serves as a splendid commentary on the text on which we are about to meditate, a text which overwhelms us by what it has signified throughout all generations of Christians, beginning with the commentaries of the Fathers and coming from the baptismal catechesis of the early church all the way down to us.

We Are Baptized into Moses

Before we deal with our text directly, however, I would like to mention that St. Paul already had his Christians meditate on it:

> I want you to be quite certain, brothers, that our ancestors all had the cloud over them and all passed through the sea. In the cloud and in the sea they were all baptised into Moses (1 Cor 10:1-2).

He believes that all Israel has passed through the sea. For that reason, Christians recalling the sentiments of the *Haggadah* of the Hebrew Pasch ought to add: "We too were there; we too have been baptized with our ancestors." In brief, the experience of the baptism that we have received in Christ is joined to what our ancestors have experienced. In meditating on their baptism, we are not reflecting on an experience foreign to us but on the origin, the meaning and the type of our fundamental baptismal experience. Here I would like to call attention to the odd phrase, "they were all baptized *into Moses*" (*kai pantes eis ton Mousēn ebaptisthesan*), just as we have been baptized in Christ. In this meditation we shall ask ourselves what the expression "they were all baptized into Moses" means, since St. Paul uses it so forcibly.

In the New Testament there is another very beautiful and important passage in which the journey under the guidance of Moses is interpreted as a journey of faith:

> It was by faith that he [Moses] left Egypt without fear of the king's anger; he held to his purpose like someone who could see the Invisible. It was by faith that he kept *the Passover* and sprinkled *the blood* to prevent *the Destroyer* from touching dry land, while the Egyptians, trying to do the same, were drowned (Heb 11:27-29).

The author of the Letter to the Hebrews intends to affirm the continuity between the faith of Christians today and that of our ancestors.

Now after that introduction, I plan to present this meditation in a very simple manner, taking a cue here or there from the text without pretending to deal with it as a whole. I have entitled the first point, "The Night of Terror"; the second, "What Does Moses Do?"; the third, "The Passage Through the Sea of Reeds"; and the fourth, "The Paschal Canticle of the Baptized."

1. The Night of Terror

This first point is a commentary on Exodus 14, especially verses 10-14 which begin: "As Pharaoh approached, the Israelites looked up — and there were the Egyptians in pursuit of them! The Israelites were terrified and cried out to Yahweh for help" (Ex 14:10). We are lost! That is why I speak of a night of terror.

In order to understand better what happened when the Israelites were seized with great fear, I have devised a brief *midrash* in the style of the rabbis. It is a very simple little story, which I call "The Midrash of the Tent." Let us imagine the scene: Night falls very quickly in the desert; we are at the edge of the desert as night begins. A few hundred yards away the waves of the sea are heard rising and falling. To the left lies the encampment of the Hebrews, who are lighting the first evening fires. Everyone is busy and gesticulating; the men, gathered in small groups, are having discussions. There is something momentous in the air; the moment of tragedy seems to be approaching. Someone runs to the next camp and returns with news. The excitement grows.

We approach the encampment and, by making signs with our hands, ask for an explanation (at that time the Hebrews did not yet speak Hebrew; they learned it only later). They point to a large tent in the middle of the camp. We walk toward the tent and try to see what is happening inside. We notice a palefaced man, short of breath, silent, surrounded by other men with long beards and clenched fists. We grasp that the man must be Moses, and the others are the elders of Israel. What is Moses doing? He is standing there without saying anything and seems paralyzed. And what are the elders of Israel doing? They are talking, shouting and raving.

The Elders of Israel Speak

Now we shall try to hear their conversation. One says: "Just see, Moses, where you have led us! We believed you; we thought that God had spoken to you. And instead, we are here to die like rats. Either we hurl ourselves into the sea and drown or let ourselves be killed by Pharaoh. That's where we are! It's the end of Israel!"

Another stands up and announces: "We thought that you had

changed, Moses. We knew that you were imprudent and hard-headed, but we believed that the desert had done you good. But you've remained exactly the same as you always were and you've plunged us into disaster again."

A third speaks up: "Brothers, listen to me. We have arms. [In fact, Exodus 13:19 says, "The Israelites left Egypt fully armed."] It's true that the Egyptians are very powerful, but if we march against them, at least our history will have a glorious ending. Let's die as heroes and praise Yahweh as we fall with our weapons in our hands!"

A fourth, more venerable than the others, intervenes: "Brothers, listen to me. I have much experience of life. I know Moses well, and I didn't have much confidence in him either, even when he returned from the desert. I had him sized up as a dreamer. Anyway, listen to me. I know Pharaoh; he isn't wicked. Moreover, he needs us and therefore has no intention of exterminating our people. On the contrary, he is very interested in reinstating us in our former situation. Let's be humble and not tempt God. Our present position is intolerable. Let's send a message to Pharaoh. Moses should not let himself be seen. Instead, some of our wise men should go and say to Pharaoh: 'We have sinned, receive us again, we are ready to turn back. We relied on this man, but he deceived us.' " Then this old man's tone becomes even more persuasive and forceful: "Brothers, listen to me! Pharaoh means security, peace and bread for our children. Don't reject this chance; don't be foolish!"

Still another rises to ask: "And supposing that God really did speak to Moses? What will we do? Will we go against God?"

But another contradicts him: "No, that's not possible. God cannot abandon his people. Our situation is desperate. How can this desperation be God's will?"

That is what is happening in this tent. On the one side, there is Moses; on the other, there is Pharaoh with his threats but also with his promises and with what he signifies in the way of a reasonable and just solution to the complex situations of life. In the middle are the elders, divided between Moses and Pharaoh. At the moment, those favoring Pharaoh are in the ascendancy, while only a few dare to defend Moses.

Which of the Two?

Reflecting on this scene I again ask myself: "Who is Pharaoh, and who is Moses?" Pharaoh represents an accommodating and accommodated life that allows for the compromises necessary to guarantee a certain tranquillity. It is a life in which we can manage to have it both ways, in which we can uphold our profession of faith and our Christian vocation exteriorly while conducting ourselves in such a way that we are not too exposed. Therefore we adjust ourselves to certain externals and securities that offer us protection in any case. In brief, Pharaoh embodies here an accommodation to a worldly kind of peace, an equilibrium attained by a shrewd dosage of following the Lord combined with a certain sense of security that we are not willing to renounce. So we strike the happy medium. Since at heart Pharaoh is reasonable, he will accept this compromise and now and then let us go out to offer sacrifice in the desert. This Pharaoh actually typifies the temptation of everyone in this world. And here each of us would do well to reflect on what this Pharaoh of reasonable compromises and tranquillity concretely signifies in our life.

Now who is Moses? Moses is the insecurity of following Jesus, that insecurity on which the Lord seems to insist by provoking and challenging those who step forward to follow him. There are so many people of good will who desire to follow Jesus, but he treats them harshly.

> One of the scribes then came up and said to him, "Master, I will follow you wherever you go." Jesus said, "Foxes have holes and the birds of the air have nests, but the Son of man has nowhere to lay his head."
>
> Another man, one of the disciples, said to him, "Lord, let me go and bury my father first." But Jesus said, "Fol-

low me, and leave the dead to bury their dead" (Mt 8:19-20).

Jesus becomes provocative, almost as though he wants to offend. Moses does the same at the Sea of Reeds; he proposes to Israel a difficult and clear-cut choice devoid of any security.

The Challenge of Our Faith

Moses stands for the insecurity that is in store for those who accept the challenge of life according to the gospel. This evangelical way of life is a blow to the world and to all our attempts to establish some nice quiet corners for ourselves. It is the challenge of faith whose sting we forcefully feel whenever we find ourselves in surroundings where there are only a few Christians — or none but ourselves — and the question arises: "How is it that all the others are making life comfortable for themselves and enjoying themselves as much as they can? And I'm supposed to sacrifice myself? What for?"

The fact is that people instinctively endeavor to be well off, to enjoy things, to settle down and acquire as much as they can of all kinds of goods for themselves. The challenge of faith is felt more strongly precisely when we are among those for whom only this life counts and we find ourselves alone in believing that this life is not the only one there is. It is then that we feel lonely, abandoned and alienated. This is the challenge of faith that is painful for us wherever unbelievers are in the majority and their opinions hold sway, determining the atmosphere and becoming a power. This is the challenge of Moses! In order to better understand the impact of this challenge, let us meditate on the following scene in the light of this episode of Moses. Jesus on the cross is mocked and insulted:

> The passers-by jeered at him; they shook their heads and said, "So you would destroy the Temple and in three days rebuild it! Then save yourself if you are God's son and come down from the cross!" The chief priests with the scribes and elders mocked him in the same way, with the

words, "He saved others; he cannot save himself. He is the king of Israel; let him come down from the cross now, and we will believe in him. He has put his trust in God; now let God rescue him if he wants him. For he did say, 'I am God's son' " (Mt 27:39-43).

The priests and the elders are practically contradicting their own good judgment when they say of Jesus: "Look at what he has come to! And he wanted the people to believe in him. It's good that we could prevent such foolishness. If he ended up like this, how could God have been with him? We knew what had to be said to the people." Moses — like Jesus — was exposed to contradiction at its utmost with the accusation: "God is not with him. But he is with us."

By Way of Contrast

Summarizing the first point, we can say that Pharaoh typifies life according to the spirit of the world. As we have already mentioned, this spirit is found everywhere; for instance, wherever we make a sect out of the church or regard our community as something that possesses its own glory within itself. The spirit of the world urges us to transfer our hopes from the word of God to the works that we aim to accomplish at all costs. Such a frame of mind is inevitably rather sectarian. Not having placed sufficient confidence in the hope that God alone gives, we endeavor to rely on something that represents us, something with which we can identify in order to find our security in it.

Moses, on the contrary, symbolizes life according to the gospel, based solely on the word of God. It is a life that does not admit of compromise. That is the irreducible contrast between the two ways of life.

2. What Does Moses Do?

In our *midrash* Moses has kept silence until now. Let us try to look into his heart where a thousand thoughts are whirring.

What could Moses have done? I would say that he had four main possibilities before him.

The Possible Choices

The *first* possibility would have been to abscond. He could have proposed: "Brothers, what you have said is very important and worth careful consideration. Return to your tents and give me an hour's time. Then we shall meet again." In the meantime he could have slipped away and gone back to the desert. This is what some politicians do once they have brought the people to the brink of disaster. They disappear from the scene by committing suicide. In fact, the temptation to suicide is not as rare as one would think.

The *second* option could consist in arming the people, as some had advised: "Let us take up arms and die as heroes!" It is the choice that falsely interprets the gospel as heroism, as though the gospel called us to fight doggedly, to resist with every ounce of our strength, and so to leave a glorious name behind — a worldly and pharaonic glory.

The *third* possibility could be to organize the return to Egypt and suggest: "Brothers, you are right. I am the only one who can propose this course of action to the Israelites; they will listen to me. Let us send a legation and negotiate."

Finally, the *fourth* choice: to trust in God and pray, "Lord, you brought me here; you will act." It is an almost wild possibility because it means not doing anything. Moses could have been thinking, "And what if God decides not to help me? Then everything will come crashing down upon me." Precisely this is the faith that is being required of Moses. It is a matter of opening himself to the unknown designs of God. Notice the dramatic character of this final possibility, which becomes especially painful when others are involved who demand concrete and immediate decisions of the pharaonic kind. Faith, however, requires a different decision, a frightening one. If Moses had armed everyone, it would have been disastrous, but at least something would have been undertaken and anxiety overcome. How much more terrifying it is in this situation of insupportable anguish to say instead, "The Lord has spoken; the Lord will show himself." Even to surrender by organizing a return to Pharaoh, however humiliating it would be, would still have been less agonizing than to abandon oneself in faith. And here I would recall — with all the analogies and differences pertaining to it — the agony of Jesus in the garden. He too could have said: "I give up. I will go away. I cannot go through with it; I will not." Or he could have followed Peter's advice to take up arms and die with his disciples. Instead, Jesus chose the agony so that God's action might be manifest.

Moses Is Divided

What does Moses do then? He does what he is capable of doing — he maneuvers. In my opinion, Moses, like anyone else, manifests two facets in this choice. He is courageous and at the same time afraid, and he acts out both.

His courageous face is the one which, with God's grace, he puts on before the people, because the Lord places words of courage in his heart. When the people cry out:

> "Was it for lack of graves in Egypt, that you had to lead us out to die in the desert? What was the point of bringing us out of Egypt? Did we not tell you as much in Egypt? Leave us alone, we said, we would rather work for the Egyptians! We prefer to work for the Egyptians than to die in the desert!" (Ex 14:11-12).

Moses responds:

> "Do not be afraid! Stand firm, and you will see what Yahweh will do to rescue you today: the Egyptians you see today you will never see again" (Ex 14:13).

And then the very beautiful conclusion:

> "Yahweh will do the fighting for you; all you need to do is to keep calm" (Ex 14:14).

On the other hand, it is undeniable that Moses also had his fears. In fact, immediately following the courageous words above, the biblical account continues, "Yahweh then said to Moses, 'Why cry out to me?' " (Ex 14:15). This shows that while Moses was telling the people to remain calm, he himself was crying out to the Lord. Nor was his fear by any means minimal since in another passage in Exodus we find Moses invoking the Lord's help with the words, "How am I to deal with this people? Any moment now they will stone me!" (Ex 17:4). On the one hand, therefore, Moses follows the promptings of the Spirit urging him on to the courage of faith; on the other, he is oppressed by anxiety which drives him toward desperation. In this way he is divided.

3. The Passage Through the Sea of Reeds

As Moses cries out to the Lord, his faith is being purified. The result is that the Lord himself intervenes:

> "Tell the Israelites to march on. Your part is to raise your
> staff and stretch out your hand over the sea and divide it,
> so that the Israelites can walk through the sea on dry
> ground" (Ex 14:15-16).

Then the scene of the passage through the sea is described. It all unfolds in a dignified and solemn manner, as though it were a royal procession. Israel advances during the night, as if to demonstrate how easy God makes things when we leave them to him, abandon them completely to him and say: "Here I am, Lord, ready to do your will. I do not understand anything, but I know that this trial you are sending me surely makes sense. I offer you my life. I desire to follow you in poverty, that is, without human means and human success." Then things develop with exemplary simplicity, without the frenetic, spasmodic anxiety of the Israelites with their proposals to fight to the death or send envoys. The night of terror becomes the night of peace and tranquillity.

They Trust in Him

What does St. Paul mean when he says that the Israelites "were baptized into Moses"? It indicates that they trusted in him. Relying on Moses, they entered the sea: "God has spoken to him. So, forward! It is terrifying to advance under cover of night along a strip of land walled by waves on both sides, but we let ourselves be led by Moses because we have placed our trust in him." For the Israelites, to be baptized into Moses meant to take Moses' risk and insecurity upon themselves. In the same way, for us to be baptized in Jesus signifies taking the risk of Jesus upon ourselves and saying to him: "Lord, I will follow you wherever you go. I want to live like you live, eat like you eat, sleep like you sleep, face the same disappointments as you." This entails deciding to lead a paschal life, a life according to the Spirit, that is, to allow ourselves to be saved by the Spirit of Jesus.

In following Moses the Israelites decided to leave everything to God, to let themselves be carried as though "on eagle's wings" (Ex 19:4). In following Jesus we choose to let him save us. We place our confidence in his infinite power, in his wisdom and ability to lead us; we permit ourselves to be immersed in him, voluntarily assuming his risks and his insecurities day by day. We accept the possibility of becoming fulfilled, affectively and culturally, or of being crushed by small and paltry situations. We run the risk of Jesus without seeking our own fulfillment, which would only be another pharaonic undertaking. Then we understand the importance of the words, "Yahweh will do the fighting for you; all you need to do is to keep calm." It is the Lord who makes the basic decision. It is his work. To be baptized in him is to let ourselves be invaded by the power of the Spirit.

4. The Paschal Canticle of the Baptized

The canticle found in Exodus 15 is one of the most ancient biblical compositions. We could call it "The Canticle of the Baptized," the canticle of those who, having agreed to take upon themselves the risk of Jesus and having staked their own lives on the gospel against all worldly evidence, can marvel: "How simple it all was! The Lord carried us almost without our noticing it. We saw the Egyptians fall. We were crazed with fear of them, the most powerful people in the world, and instead it was their corpses that were floating on the water." To sum up, once we have made the unreserved decision to let the Spirit of the Lord invade us, all the conditionings that caused such intense fear gradually show themselves to be as nothing. At the same time, life in the spirit of the gospel appears simple, easy and beautiful.

Let us listen to the Canticle of Moses (Exodus 15):

> I shall sing to Yahweh, for he has covered himself in glory,
> horse and rider he has thrown into the sea.
>
> *—I was afraid of horses that run faster than I, and of the riders armed with lances.—*
>
> Yah is my strength and my song,
> to him I owe my deliverance.
> He is my God and I shall praise him,
> my father's God and I shall extol him.
>
> *—Now everything is submerged in the Sea: Pharaoh's chariots and his whole army, all that power which terrified me, all those obstacles that arose before me (objections such as, "You will not be able to do it," "It will be an impossible life," "You will have to go against modern ideas," "Your life will no longer be authentic"), all that anxiety, often under the guise of psychology or sociology ("To live like that doesn't make sense," "Your personality won't develop . . . ").*

67

The ocean has closed over them;
they have sunk to the bottom like a stone.

—*Without my having done anything!*—

Your right hand, Yahweh, wins glory by its strength,
your right hand, Yahweh, shatters your foes.

This is the canticle of the baptized who know themselves to be saved and say, "God has fought for me. I said yes to the Spirit, and the Lord did everything else."

Let us ask the Lord to make us understand that our decision for the gospel, which ought to be renewed every day, is so simple.

Moses, the Servant of God

In the Book of Numbers Moses is called "servant":

Not so with my servant Moses;
    to him my whole household is entrusted"
    (Nm 12:7).

This title — servant — is repeated at the moment of Moses' death: "Moses, the servant of Yahweh, died as Yahweh decreed" (Dt 34:5). It is a title of honor bestowed on him at the end of his life. The Letter to the Hebrews quotes Numbers almost verbatim in order to show that although Moses attained the dignity of servant, he is nothing compared to Jesus, who is Son:

It is true that Moses was *trustworthy in the household* of God, as a *servant* is, acting as witness to the things which were yet to be revealed, but Christ is trustworthy as a son is, over his household (Heb 3:5-6).

A Commentary of St. Gregory of Nyssa

Toward the end of his *Life of Moses*, Gregory of Nyssa gives a magnificent commentary on this description of Moses as a faithful servant, a man of trust. In a sentence that covers a page and a half, Gregory, a master of oratorical technique, presents a brilliant sample of all his skills. I shall now cite a passage:

We learn something from the fact that after having endured so many labors, Moses was finally judged worthy to be called by the sublime name of *servant of God*, which is equivalent to being superior to all.

Then he continues:

> What do we learn from this? To have only one aim in this life; that of being called *servants of God* on the basis of our deeds.

And relative to this title, in that one long sentence he then summarizes the whole story of Moses, applying it to "you who are reading":

> In fact, when you have triumphed over all your enemies — the Egyptians, the Amalekites, the Edomites, the Medianites; when you have passed through the water; when you have been enlightened by the cloud; when you have rendered the water potable by means of the wood; when you have drunk from the rock; when you have savored the food from above; when you have travelled the way that leads you to the mountain; or when you have been instructed in the divine mysteries . . . [continuing in this manner, the whole life of Moses is applied to the reader] . . . when you have reduced to nothing all that revolts, like Dathan, against your dignity, consuming it with fire like Korah was consumed [he refers here to the last episodes of revolt, which Moses suppressed], then you will be approaching the end, and by this word "end" I mean that in view of which everything happens: thus, the end of cultivating the fields is to taste the fruits; the end of building a house is to live in it; the end of all commerce is to grow rich; and finally the end of the exertions in the stadium is to win the crown; and so the end of the spiritual life is to be called *servants of God*.

The Centrality of Service in Our Life

I would like to suggest some reflections on this subject that I regard as fundamental, because what we seek is not merely a prolonged time of prayer or some kind of experience of God, however lovely these may be, but prayer and experience of God with a view to discerning what to choose in order to serve better. This learning how to serve better implies, therefore, learning how to be more available and more aware of the real needs of our brothers and sisters and of the church. To put it briefly, if I had to crystallize in a question the theme of this meditation, I would ask: "Where does the passage through the Sea of Reeds lead us?" It certainly does not bring us to an easy and secure life, but rather to a genuine gospel life. And in what does this life consist? As we shall see, it is a life of service (*diakonia*), a life expended for others.

Here let us recall again the rabbinical wisdom which anticipated all this. I have already quoted the text about the three periods in the life of Moses: of Hillel the Elder, of Rabban Johnathan Ben Zakai and of Rabbi Akiba. You will recall that these men had spent the first 40 years of their lives in various activities. Then they passed the second 40 years in what was described as "serving the sages." This consisted in learning the Torah in order to acquire a culture of their own and become good rabbis. Finally it is related that in the third 40-year period all four served Israel for 40 years. Hence this was the goal of their entire formation and the culmination of their careers.

In this meditation I extracted a few suggestions from the many passages of the Pentateuch and divided them into three reflections or points. The first reflection gleans from the pages of Exodus, Numbers and Deuteronomy the various services that Moses rendered his people, beginning with the passage through the Sea of Reeds. The second is an analysis of Christian life as a life of service. The third point, much briefer than the others, takes into consideration the various successive steps and different stages of this service.

1. The Services Rendered by Moses

I have tried to bring together the various episodes recounted in the Pentateuch and to synthesize them roughly into five types of service that Moses exercised. They appear in a certain order, which seems to me to progress from the lesser to the greater, even though the lesser is very important and basic. They are: the service of bread and water, of responsibility, of prayer and intercession, of consolation and of the word.

The Service of Bread and Water

The canticle has hardly been sung and the enthusiasm over passing through the Sea of Reeds hardly died down when the people begin to murmur because they do not find water (Ex 15:22). So Moses is forced to begin with this. The poor man had never dreamed of becoming a manager, and now he has to become involved even in this kind of problem. Immediately thereafter, as though inadvertently, the account continues by saying that bread is wanting (Ex 16:3-4), and consequently Moses has to be concerned about this too. Afterward meat is lacking and then again water (Ex 16:8—17:7). Thus the first service which Moses has to render is an elementary one, that of providing water, bread and meat. When he heard the Lord's voice commissioning him — "Go and free my people" — he never thought he would have to perform this kind of service.

In fact, his father-in-law, Jethro, a wise man, will say to him:

> "Why do you do this for the people, why sit here alone with the people standing round you from morning till evening?" Moses replied to his father-in-law, "Because the people come to me to consult God. When they have a problem they come to me, and I give a ruling between the one and the other and make God's statutes and laws known to them." Moses' father-in-law then said to him, "What you are doing is not right. You will only tire yourself out, and the people with you too, for the work is too heavy for

you. You cannot do it all yourself. Now listen to the advice
I am going to give you, and God be with you!" (Ex 18:14-
19).

Then Jethro teaches him the principle of subsidiarity by suggest-
ing that he select some upright elders and appoint them as lead-
ers of groups of a thousand, a hundred, fifty and ten. Only the
more important problems would be reserved to Moses. "If you
do this — and may God so command you — you will be able to
stand the strain, and all these people will go home satisfied"
(Ex 19:23). This is a very important moment in Moses' life, for
he had to learn how to exercise authority. In the beginning, in
his inexperience, he thought he could do everything, but he
learned differently. This incident is so important that it is mentioned in Deuteronomy which repeats the story of Moses' life
(Dt 1:9 18).

In any event, although at a certain point Moses learned that he
could not do everything himself, it remains true that with God's
providence he was able to learn to do something of everything.
In other words, he made himself personally accountable for all
the people's needs and thereby discovered that there are essential
needs and necessary services. In this way he became a great re-
alist and perhaps lost a bit of his idealism and that dash of intel-
lectualism to which he could have been tempted after spending
40 years in the desert communing with the stars. He realized
that there are urgent needs which must be attended to without
delay for the people are crying out and are hungry. In Moses'
formation for ministry it is very important that the Lord lets him
be exposed to this kind of service. Later the Lord does the same
for the apostles in Jerusalem, as the Acts of the Apostles relates.
At a certain point, after having undergone the formation im-
posed on them by prolonged serving at table, they see that they
cannot continue and decided to appoint deacons for this purpose
(Acts 6).

The Service of Responsibility

Moses feels the burden of this service very much. It is as though he carries his people on his shoulders, with their defects and immaturity. Gradually he comes to understand how necessary it is to accept people as they are, with all their grumbling, restlessness and outbursts of anger. It is as he himself says in his autobiography:

> "At the same time, I told you, 'I cannot be responsible for you [the people] by myself. Yahweh your God has increased your numbers' " (Dt 1:9-10).

Here Moses clearly shows that he is convinced of his obligation to carry the burden of the people. Then he adds, "So how can I cope by myself with the bitter burden that you are, and with your bickering?" (Dt 1:12).

Moses knows very well that he has to bear the pressure, the cares and the disagreements of the people as they are — quarrelsome people. Besides all the other problems that life in the desert brings, they will perhaps contend for a single tent or a spot of ground and claim Moses' intervention. In this way he has learned to assume the service of responsibility. And as we are aware, it is not merely the service of those holding official responsibility but of each one of us insofar as we are responsible for one another. Each of us is responsible for those whom we know, for their problems and burdens, and thus we mutually support one another. It is the service that Moses exercised to the utmost that is a model for us.

The Service of Prayer and Intercession

Moses discharges this third service too at his own expense. We speak here not only of the intercession that consists in putting in a good word for someone. Moses is always personally involved in what he says. As a typical example of prayer and intercession, think of the incident in which Moses raises his hands in the battle against the Amalekites:

> As long as Moses kept his arms raised, Israel had the advantage; when he let his arms fall, the advantage went to Amalek. But Moses' arms grew heavy, — [yes, the service of prayer is fatiguing!] — so they took a stone and put it under him and on this he sat, with Aaron and Hur supporting his arms on each side. Thus his arms remained unwavering until sunset (Ex 17:11-12).

This picture of Moses praying until sundown is very beautiful. It is a portrait of the church's great intercessors, a source of inspiration for the contemplatives as they intercede for humanity.

In his ministry of intercession Moses dares much. On the other hand, his profound knowledge of God allows him to use words that seem almost blasphemous to us. When the Lord is angry with his people on account of the golden calf, Moses says to him, "This people has committed a great sin by making themselves a god of gold." (Ex 32:31). Here he acknowledges the state of affairs without trying to cover it up with a lie, as Adam did. "And yet, if it pleased you to forgive their sin . . . ! If not, please blot me out of the book you have written!" (Ex 32:32). Moses lives the experience of his people as one of them, to the point of wanting to be afflicted by God himself just to intercede for them. Evidently this is a rare case, similar to the one in which Paul says, "I could pray that I myself might be accursed and cut off if this could benefit the brothers who are my own flesh and blood" (Rom 9:3). Nevertheless, it expresses well the degree of involvement that Moses brings into his prayer.

The rabbis not only wrote on this involvement but did so with a touch of humor. Among the legends about Moses there is one particularly astonishing account. According to this *midrash*,

> Only by contending with the people as well as against God did Moses become a man of God. Indeed, he fulfilled [here we detect something of the modern author who is speaking] two truly difficult roles: he represented God before Israel and Israel before God. When the angels spoke

against Israel — and it often happened — it was sufficient reason for Moses to silence them. When God decided to give the law to Israel as a gift, the angels objected, but Moses rebuked them: "But who is going to obey the law — you? Only men can accept the law and live according to its precepts!" And when the people hit the bottom of the abyss, dancing around the golden calf, Moses again found a way to defend them: "Is it their fault or yours, Lord? Israel has lived so long in exile among idolaters that it has been corrupted. Is it their fault if they cannot forget so easily?" He meets the divine threat by giving an ultimatum. "Either forgive everything or cross my name out of your book." And when God says to him, "Your people has sinned," Moses replies, "When Israel observes the law it is your people, and when it breaks the law, is it supposed to be mine?"

From this, we see the extent to which Moses identifies himself with his people.

The Service of Consolation

A typical case of the service of consolation is narrated on the occasion of the departure from Egypt. When the people protest: "Leave us alone . . . .We prefer to work for the Egyptians than to die in the desert," Moses responds, "Do not be afraid! Stand firm, and you will see what Yahweh will do to rescue you today: the Egyptians you see today you will never see again!" (Ex 14:12-13). Here we could reflect at length on this consoling intervention, which is not a vague "Go in peace, be calm, take courage," but a very precise word that effectively encourages in the name of God. It is a service rendered in faith and not mere human sympathy.

The Service of the Word

Even though we shall not meditate here on the *Halakah* of Moses — all the prescriptions, laws and precepts that fill the books of Exodus and Leviticus — we can say that the service of the word is what primarily marks Moses as the man of the word of God. We know that the greater part of Moses' mission consists in announcing the word to the people. It is his basic mission, which according to Sirach essentially distinguishes him:

[God] allowed him to hear his voice,
and led him into the darkness;
he gave him the commandments face to face,
the law of life and knowledge,
to teach Jacob his ordinances
and Israel his decrees (Sir 45:5-6).

We could also mention the passage in which the great service of the word originates: "Moses then went up to God, and Yahweh called to him from the mountain, saying, 'Say this to the House of Jacob! Tell the Israelites' " (Ex 19:3). Here the Decalogue and the whole law is being referred to. From now on Moses will live at the service of the word that God entrusted to him to convey to the people.

2. Christian Life, a Life of Service

What do we mean in saying that a paschal life according to the gospel — the life of those who have passed through the Sea of Reeds — is a life spent in service to others, a ministry of service? We shall attempt to answer this question by comparing the two figures of Moses and Jesus and then drawing the right conclusions.

Becoming Like Moses

As Gregory of Nyssa so well says, Christian life entails becoming like Moses. The sentence from the Letter to the Hebrews, which we have already quoted, succinctly expresses all that Moses was: "A servant, trustworthy in the household of

God" (Heb 3:5). Let us now endeavor to understand the meaning of this statement word by word.

He was a servant in the various ways that we have just commented on. In this text, *trustworthy* does not merely mean that he faithfully fulfilled his work; rather, it has the sense of being reliable. Others can entrust themselves to him because, as we have seen, he is completely one with Israel. If Moses had had his own plans and personal whims, he could not have been trusted, but because he identifies himself entirely with Israel, the Lord can entrust him with this people. In this connection, we can recall those in the church who stand out because of their availability for service. Not having any agenda of their own, they are available for whatever the Lord wants to do through them. Take, for instance, Pope John XXIII with his motto "Obedience and Peace." He accepted whatever the church assigned to him, and from then on his sole aim was to minister to the kingdom of God in its needs from day to day. Each one of us has known or knows people in the church to whom anything can be entrusted because they identify themselves with whatever is delegated to them. That is how Moses was — completely trustworthy. His plan and God's had become identical.

And he deserved this trust "in the household of God." He was qualified for every kind of service, from the service of food to that of the word. Moses had his own personal talents, and we know that he was probably not so clever in speaking. Nevertheless he took this upon himself also when the Lord chose him for it.

Inserted Into God's Plan

The text says: "in the *household*." This indicates that Moses considered the people not as a structure or a bureaucratic organism but as a house, a family. Still more, he himself was one of the family and lived within God's plan as though in a familiar ambient, marked by relationships of confidence which surpass those that can be labelled. While it is true that even labels have their function, it is certain that no one could ever have categorized Moses. If someone had asked him, "Are you a prophet, a leader of the people or a seer?" he would have responded, "I do not know. I just do what God asks of me." It is impossible to tag Moses, because he is inserted into God's plan just as it is. I say this not because I discredit order and regularity in things, but because sometimes we are inclined to close ourselves off. We discharge our duty without bothering about others. This makes sense if it means to avoid meddling in the affairs of others. But in the depths of our soul we should maintain an availability for everything that humanity and the church require of us. Without this sense of co-responsibility for the needs of all the others in our hearts, there is no spiritual discernment of our various Christian vocations.

To return to our text now — "in the household *of God*"; in God's house, not in the house of Moses. This is important. The first Moses would have wanted to establish his own house and would have envisioned making a major power out of the people. The later Moses so identifies himself with the people that he risks being rejected by God. But he can risk such an excommunication because he is so convinced that the work is God's and not his own. From its very inception onward, he regards it as *of* God. How true this is can be seen if we meditate on Moses' death. When God says to him, "Now, die," Moses actually dies. The Lord has declared that he may not continue, because his task is finished. From now on others will lead the people forward, and the Lord will conduct them to the other side of the Jordan. From this it is evident that Moses identified himself with the people as a people; he did not seek his own glory but God's.

Called to Service Like Jesus

Christian life, then, consists in becoming like Moses, with him and in the same manner as he did, being protagonists of a life of service. In reality, those who follow the example of

Moses find that they are *like Jesus*, the servant without equal. Here I shall cite two texts to demonstrate that the New Testament conceives of Jesus' life as one of service. In the first passage Jesus is being spoken of, while in the second he speaks of himself.

> *You wanted no sacrifice or cereal offering,*
> *but you gave me a body.*
> *You took no pleasure in burnt offering or*
> *   sacrifice for sin;*
> *then I said, "Here I am, I am coming,"*
> *in the scroll of the book it is written of me,*
> *to do your will, God.* (Heb 10:5-7).

The author concludes:

> And this *will* [to sacrifice and to serve unstintingly] was for us to be made holy by the *offering* of the *body* of Jesus Christ made once and for all (Heb 10:10).

The second text is a passage from Mark which we could call theological in the sense that Mark normally reports deeds of Jesus rather than focusing on his words as Matthew and Luke do. Nevertheless, Mark has not by-passed these words of Jesus: "For the Son of man himself came not to be served but to serve, and to give his life as a ransom for many" (Mk 10:45). Jesus says this in order to admonish the apostles that they too ought to be servants. Thus Jesus' life of service is to be transferred to the life of every Christian. To be like Moses and like Jesus is to be called to service.

Concretely speaking, what does it mean to be called to serve? It is to pass openly and courageously from Pharaoh to Moses. In this case Pharaoh stands for possessiveness, letting our projects be centered on ourselves. Moses, on the other hand, is the humble servant who is concerned about making himself useful to others, forgetting himself, in the spirit of Jesus, who taught that only those who are willing to die will live.

This, then, is Christian *diakonia*; it is a total service, embracing the whole person and all of humanity. It is total because it binds our whole personality. As Paul affirms, a diaconal mentality ponders day and night trying to discover humanity's true needs as well as what it would have to do in order to serve these needs better. We cannot live as Christians and at the same time prescind from this service of the *whole person*, from the needs of men and women in this world: the need for bread, meat, consolation, intercession and the word. Obviously I am speaking of Christian service in general terms which, however, become specific according to the various charisms, as Paul insists. But the fact remains that the church, as the diaconal assembly of the baptized, ought to be open to needs of all kind, to the needs of all, beginning with the more evident and urgent necessities down to those that are deeper and more serious, though perhaps less apparent.

3. Steps and Stages in a Life of Service

As we have seen, a life dedicated to service demands totality. But we often make the mistake of wanting to do everything. This is presumption, for it is as church that we are called to serve. Therefore we need to be woven into the fabric of the church and then within the church gradually discern the steps and stages of our service. At times we are apt to think that everyone needs us, whereas in reality each one of us can contribute only a very small share. But it would be absurd to think that we can accomplish even this minimal part if we are not inserted into the context of a church whose lifeblood is service, and if we do not participate in a certain rhythm of formation, preparation, selection and distribution of tasks. Otherwise we would make the same mistake as Moses did at first, when he tried to do everything himself. Since there are so many others with us, we ought to look around to see what each one can do.

At the conclusion of this meditation, let us ask the Lord to grant us the true spirit of service.

Sixth Meditation

Moses, "Propheta Traditus"

The theme of this meditation will be the so-called passion of Moses. For this purpose we shall keep in mind the typological connection between Moses and Jesus that the New Testament presents: The involvement of Moses leads to suffering and that of Jesus leads to death; Jesus, the suffering servant, corresponds to Moses, the suffering servant. On the other hand, we already know that Moses is called the "servant of Yahweh," probably the four well-known Songs of the Servant of Yahweh in Deutero-Isaiah took their inspiration from Moses and at the same time pointed toward a future mysterious messianic personage. Now we have three figures before us: the suffering Moses, the servant of Yahweh (of whom we cannot speak at length here), and finally, Jesus facing his passion.

In the title of this meditation I have used the Latin expression *"propheta traditus"* because the Latin verb *tradere* so adequately renders the three accepted meanings of the Greek verb *paradidonai* that the New Testament uses in referring to Jesus. We shall examine an instance of each of these meanings. In Peter's discourse near Solomon's portico, he declares, "It is *the God of Abraham, Isaac and Jacob, the God of our ancestors, who has glorified his servant* Jesus, whom you handed over *(paredokate)*" (Acts 3:13). You delivered him up and disowned him before Pilate, Peter says. Jesus is handed over, *traditus*, by humankind, by us.

In Romans the same verb indicates the action of the Father: "After saying this, what can we add? If God is for us, who can be against us? Since he who did not spare his own son, but gave him up (*paredoken auton*) for the sake of all of us . . . " (Rom 8:31-32). Hence the Father delivered Jesus into our hands that we might do with him what we wanted — that we might accept him, adore him and love him. But our freedom also placed us in a position where we could choose not to love and accept him; we were free to reject him, to oppose him and even to put him to death. Nevertheless the Father delivered him over to humanity.

The third meaning of our verb appears in Galatians 2:20, where Christ himself is the subject: "I am alive; yet it is no longer I, but Christ living in me. The life that I am now living, subject to the limitation of human nature, I am living in faith, faith in the Son of God who loved me and gave himself for me" (*kai paradontos eauton upèr emou*). Here it is Jesus who delivers himself up for us. By means of the intersecting of these three meanings of the one word, *tradere*, we can contemplate the mystery of the cross, the revelation of the mystery of the burning bush: 1) the Father, who freely delivers up his Son to humanity; 2) the Son, who delivers himself for our salvation; and 3) humanity, which betrays him. This truth will be the object of our meditation. We shall concentrate, however, on the figure of Moses as a type of Jesus. Moses is the prophet delivered up in the ways already mentioned: God delivers him up to the people, he delivers himself up to his people and the people make him suffer. Moses does not go so far as to die; he does not give his life. It is Jesus who gives his life. But in his body Moses will suffer rejection by the people. In the first part of our meditation, therefore, we shall examine some situations in which Moses suffered. Then, in the second part, I shall recall for you some analogous — or different but corresponding — situations in which Jesus suffered. Moses' suffering will help us to contemplate and better understand the profundity of Jesus' love. Then it will be up to us to deeply contemplate the mystery of the Father who gives the Son and of the Son who freely gives himself, despite our betrayal, and continues to give himself notwithstanding our rejection.

1. The Sufferings of Moses

Among the many narrations in Exodus and Numbers that describe the various trials of Moses, I have selected four and entitled them as follows: Moses' levity, his fear, his insecurity and his patience. As an introduction to these points, I would like to quote a few passages from Andre Neher, a Jewish classical author on this subject. In 1955 Neher published a book on the essence of prophetism in which, with keen insight, he attempted to formulate the phenomenology of the prophetic experience within the framework of the history of religions. Regarding Moses, he writes:

> A new experience, one which Abraham did not know, characterizes Moses as prophet. It is an experience that introduces an essential element into biblical prophetism: Moses is the first to feel the *suffering* of the prophetic vocation. Abraham accepts all the divine offers with unwavering equanimity. He leaves the country of the Chaldeans, makes the journeys imposed on him by the Lord and confronts difficulties. Even in the description of the sacrifice of his son, there is not a word about what he is feeling. It is as though he undergoes everything with absolute faith. He is the prophet of certainty. Moses, on the contrary, is the prophet of doubt, of rejection, of revolt. It is to him that we repeatedly turn when we look for the example of a prophecy in *sorrow*.

Thus Neher makes Abraham the direct opposite of Moses: *"Abraham est un prophète abrité. Moïse est un prophète livré"* — Abraham is a sheltered prophet; Moses is a prophet delivered

up. This is the difference between the two: "With Moses, revelation assumes a more tragic character." Then the author questions why this tragic aspect of the service of the word, of proph-
ecy, is emphasized in the case of Moses and not of Abraham.
And he answers:

> It derives from the fact that a prophet in the style of Abra-
> ham is an individual, while one in the style of Moses is in-
> serted into the history of a people. Abraham is the prophet
> standing alone; it is from him that the people is born.
> Moses' mission, on the other hand, inserts him into the
> ambient of a human community. Of necessity, then, there
> arise conflict, concrete struggle and dialogue with others.
> It is a much more difficult dialogue and one very different
> from simple dialogue with God, because it is much more
> subject to the risk of failure.

When we deal with God, any failure is experienced only in ourselves. But if we must be a prophet for others, all our activity is
exposed to their acceptance or rejection, to their indifference or
resistance. Moses is the central figure in this drama. This is so
true, says the author, that at times "when failure seems inevitable (that is, when Israel is in a state of revolt and the end of its
history seems imminent), God allows Moses the option of becoming a new Abraham, a prophet-patriarch: 'I will make of
you a new people.' " As we know, Moses reacts with, "No, I
want to continue with my people." And Neher concludes: "The
fulfillment of the revelation made to Moses depends conjointly
on his faith and the faith of the people."

This interpretation impresses me as being very profound because it likewise demonstrates the drama of Jesus: Jesus can be
accepted or rejected. He is not simply the Jesus who goes
around gloriously proclaiming the Lord. Jesus' work is the seed
that falls to the ground and is either trampled upon or eaten up
or choked, or produces fruit. These alternatives concern not
only the service of the word but all the other services as well in
the sense that they do not depend solely on those who perform

them, but also on those who receive them. Often we think that the more humble and simple services, like those of bread and water, will always be well received. But we know that this is not so. Many missionaries serving in leprosariums, for example, have been expelled from their mission country. Why? Because it was thought that everything depended only on those who intended to render a certain service. No one ever asked what the recipients thought of it, whether they really wanted it or if it indeed was the service that was most beneficial at the moment. Herein lies the reason why services offered with such courage and confidence are not accepted. The root causes of this are many. Sometimes it is due to the mistakes of those who offer their services, while at other times to the mistaken refusal of those who do not accept them. In any event, I find the interpretation proposed by Neher very valid. Moses suffers because he wants to be with the people. Had he been content to dialogue with God, he could have remained in peace, but his engagement at a certain point crushes him. In the same way Jesus' involvement with the people will cause him to be trampled on at a certain time.

Now let us endeavor to meditate on this dimension of the suffering of Moses and Jesus. First we shall look at the four episodes in Moses' life on which I invite you to reflect.

Moses' Levity

Our first scene (Ex 4:18-26) is very mysterious. Moses, obedient to the will of God,

> went back to his father-in-law Jethro and said to him, "Give me leave to return to my kinsmen in Egypt and see if they are still alive." And Jethro said to Moses, "Go in peace."
>
> . . . So Moses took his wife and his son [note that Matthew repeats this sentence in describing the return of Jesus from Egypt] and, putting them on a donkey, started

> back for Egypt; and Moses took the staff of God in his
> hand.

Filled with confidence and surrender to the Lord, Moses sets
out for Egypt with his wife and son. But,

> on the journey, when he had halted for the night, Yahweh
> encountered him and tried to kill him. Then Zipporah, tak-
> ing up a flint, cut off her son's foreskin and with it touched
> his feet and said, "You are my blood-bridegroom!" So he
> [the Lord] let him go. She said, "Blood-bridegroom,"
> then, with reference to the circumcision.

This very mysterious incident is terrifying. Even exegetes
wonder which traditions are represented here. We shall try to interpret it as it appears in its own context. Moses thought that the
call he had received had placed him more or less on his original
level: He would return to Egypt with his flocks, wife and sons
and resume a certain work. Instead the Lord desires to make
him understand that the situation has changed and that he has
taken God's words too lightly in conceiving of his mission in
this manner. Although this explanation explores only one facet
of this incident, it clearly indicates that God is letting Moses
know that his calling is not to a harmless undertaking, but rather
to something which will claim him for the rest of his life.

We can gather particularly rich lessons from this occurrence
precisely because it is so mysterious. In order to live an evangelical life and dedicate ourselves to an apostolate that is diaconal
and not pharaonic, it is not sufficient merely to make some mi-
nor changes in method or update our vocabulary. We need a
completely new attitude. We are always being tempted to reduce
the newness of the gospel — with its dynamic power to radically
change us — to a discourse on methods or procedure. But the
Lord tells us that we are dealing with a quite different matter:
"You do not have the slightest idea of what I have called you
to!" On his part, Moses now realizes that the undertaking to
which God has called him has begun in earnest, even without

his understanding it. He had cut it down to his small measure, but God stops him, even resorting to such a sensational method as he used this night.

Moses' Fear

Moses was often afraid, particularly when he realized that he could not fulfill his mission from behind the table but had to throw himself into the fray and run the same risks as the people and even greater ones. In the beginning Moses had some insight into how things should be, and therefore he tried to excuse himself: "Please, my Lord, I have never been eloquent, even since you have spoken to your servant, for I am slow and hesitant of speech" (Ex 4:10). Later, after the dialogue in which God tries to help him, when Moses realizes that what is required of him is beyond his physical strength and feels frightened at what awaits him, he finally opens his heart: "Please, my Lord, send anyone you decide to send!" (Ex 4:13) — that is, send someone else.

The prophet Isaiah will echo these words later (Is 6:4-8). But Isaiah is another type of person, and his words signify something entirely different. He means "Send me." Moses, on the contrary, claims, "I am not equal to it." Hence the Lord's anger is enkindled against him, for the exigencies of his call are not something from which Moses may retreat at will. Now that he has accepted the commission, he must persevere to the end.

Another instance of Moses' fear is manifested in his lamentation:

> "Lord, why do you treat this people so harshly? Why did you send me? Ever since I came to Pharaoh and spoke to him in your name, he has ill-treated this people, and you have done nothing at all about rescuing your people" (Ex 5:22-23).

Moses had imagined an easy liberation, but things turned out differently. Then he became afraid and asked himself, "What does God still want from me? Which way does he want to lead me?"

Still another aspect of Moses' fear is recorded: "Moses appealed to Yahweh for help. 'How am I to deal with this people?' he said. 'Any moment now they will stone me!' " (Ex 17:4). Moses' experiences have made him feel the depths of his weakness. If we wish to reflect on a New Testament text to help us to better understand Moses' anxiety, we could take a passage in which the fear of the apostles is described. When Jesus and the Twelve were on the way up to Jerusalem, "Jesus was walking on ahead of them: they were in a daze, and those who followed were apprehensive" (Mk 10:32). Jesus goes on ahead and the others follow anxiously. They wonder: "Where are we going? Where is he taking us? Why go to Jerusalem when the people there are against us?" This is the fear from which the Lord did not spare his prophets. To become a prophet and servant of the gospel does not mean to march joyfully forward filled with enthusiasm. Rather it is to suffer all the anguish of situations in which there is apparently no way out. This is how the Lord calls us to faith in his word.

Moses' Insecurity

Despite the many knocks Moses endures, he holds out — up to a certain point. Then his power of resistance seems to weaken, and he undergoes a major crisis. The Bible describes this also in mysterious and veiled language, so as to have us grasp that something serious has taken place in Moses' soul.

The incident takes place near the Waters of Meribah:

> The people laid the blame on Moses. "We would rather have died," they said, "as our brothers died before Yahweh! Why have you brought Yahweh's community into this desert, for us and our livestock to die here? Why did you lead us out of Egypt, only to bring us to this wretched place? It is a place unfit for sowing, it has no figs, no vines, no pomegranates, and there is not even water to drink!" (Nm 20:3-5).

All the people's rancor is vented against Moses and Aaron.

These two wretched men now go apart and prostrate themselves to pray. Then the Lord orders Moses:

> "Take the branch and call the community togeth-
> er. . . . Order this rock to release its water" (Nm 20:8).

So Moses takes the rod, raises his hand and says,

> "Listen now, you rebels. Shall we make water gush from this rock for you?" Moses then raised his hand and struck the rock twice with the branch; water gushed out in abundance, and the community and their livestock drank.
>
> Yahweh then said to Moses and Aaron, "Because you did not believe that I could assert my holiness before the Israelites' eyes, you will not lead this assembly into the country which I am giving them" (Nm 20:12).

This account leaves us a bit disconcerted. Moses, who has been obedient in everything until now, is overtaken by an inner crisis that is manifested in a "deficiency" whose significance remains a mystery to us. Was it perhaps his lack of faith that made him strike the rock twice? According to another tradition Moses was punished because of the people's refusal to leave Kadesh to proceed to Canaan. Moses says to them, "Yahweh was angry with me too, because of you. 'You will not go in either,' he said. 'Your assistant, Joshua the son of Nun, will be the one to enter' " (Dt 1:37-38). This text and other parallel passages (Dt 3:26; 4:21) seem to attribute Moses' punishment not so much to the episode of the waters as to his having consented to the people's desire to enter the promised Land by the route leading eastward to the Jordan rather than by that from the south. On that occasion Moses had pitied his people because they were frightened at the report that giants inhabited that area. In this way he showed lack of trust in God. I do not know which interpretation to prefer, but in any case all this is very human. We think we are progressing in virtue, when suddenly there is a downfall or a difficult moment, and we cannot cope with the pressure under which we may have been bearing up well for years. This is something to which even Moses succumbed. The moment of grave inner crisis arrived, and Moses accepted the consequences with great dignity, humility and simplicity. Moses reproaches himself for having had so much compassion on his people that he departed from God's word in order to protect them.

This is what happens when we consent to becoming involved with people. And the Lord neither promises us indefectibility nor spares us the consequences of our blunders; rather, he promises us pardon and mercy.

Moses' Patience

The final aspect that characterizes Moses' painful and humiliating engagement in the service of his people is patience. In this respect also the figure of Moses impresses us as being grand, because with all his weakness, he still manifests dedication to God and trust in him. Moses thus becomes a versatile spirit, a man of suffering.

Let us consider the following episode, rendered very interesting by Moses' psychological disposition:

> Miriam, and Aaron too, criticised Moses over the Cushite woman he had married. He had indeed married a Cushite woman. They said, "Is Moses the only one through whom Yahweh has spoken? Has he not spoken through us too?" (Nm 12:1-2).

The real reason for their speaking this way was envy, an envy that was quite disgraceful for Moses, Aaron and Miriam. They constitute the team that leads Israel but cannot agree among themselves. The situation is made still more embarrassing by the fact that it was Miriam who saved Moses from the Nile and consequently she feels somewhat protective toward him. Then,

> Yahweh said: . . .

> . . . How, then, could you dare
> to criticise my servant Moses?

> Yahweh's anger was aroused by them. He went away, and

as soon as the cloud left the Tent, there was Miriam cov-
ered with a virulent skin-disease, white as snow! Aaron
turned to look at her and saw that she had contracted a virulent skin-disease (Nm 12:6-10).

But by now Moses has learned patience; he prays that she may
be cured so that peace may be restored to the family. Here we
see Moses, the patient man, who has learned to be silent and to
let the Lord act. He bears even the most intimate suffering, that
of being misunderstood in his relationship with God by his own
family.

2. Jesus, the Suffering Servant

This second part of our meditation is devoted to applying to
Jesus, point by point, the considerations we made in the forego-
ing meditation. I shall very briefly suggest four points which,
either by contrast or by analogy, permit us to understand Jesus'
involvement with the people.

The first element is Jesus' *clearsightedness*. While Moses begins his mission with a certain jauntiness (with the ass, his wife,
his sons, the plan to spend his life out in the country), from the
very beginning Jesus knows where he is going (Lk 9:21-22).
When the crowds acclaim him for his miracles and hail his success, Jesus says, "The Son of man is destined to suffer griev-
ously." Jesus saw clearly that he would have to pay the full price
of his identification with the people, and he did not recoil from
it.

The second factor is Jesus' *fear*. This is an awesome expression, which we would never have used if it did not appear in the
gospel. Jesus is afraid and declares, "My soul is sorrowful to
the point of death" (Mk 14:34), almost like Elijah who cries
out, "Yahweh, I have had enough!" (1 Kgs 19:4). This also
shows us the parallel between Moses and Jesus: Moses was
afraid, and Jesus too was willing to experience fear in order to

93

show that serving the gospel does not exempt us from anguish in the face of catastrophic situations that can sometimes befall us.

The third characteristic, Jesus' *resoluteness*, is in contrast with Moses' insecurity at the Waters of Meribah. Jesus says of himself, "I lay down my life for my sheep" (Jn 10:15). This is perfect love joined to an attitude of complete listening to the Father. While Moses, placed between the people and God, loses his emotional balance and flares up at the people, Jesus offers his life for love of us, but in obedience to the Father's word. In this connection we can also meditate on his words, "Father, *into your hands I commit my spirit*" (Lk 23:46). Whereas Moses does not succeed in committing his spirit to God at Meribah, nor on the occasion of the tumult raised at the return of the spies, Jesus, the author of our faith, commended himself into the Father's hands for us.

In conclusion, the last quality to contemplate is Jesus' *patience*. Among the many episodes that could be cited, I have chosen that of Jesus being slapped in the face at the interrogation in the house of Annas (Jn 18:22-23). It seems to me to offer a parallel to the incident of Moses being morally boxed on the ears by Miriam and Aaron. Moses does not answer Miriam and Aaron but leaves his case to God. Jesus, on the contrary, answers, "If there is some offence in what I said, point it out; but if not, why do you strike me?" In this instance Jesus does not content himself with accepting. Instead he wants to evangelize and to offer himself as a sign of authenticity to this poor functionary, who was perhaps badly paid and full of frustrations in his constant submission, as is the case with inferiors placed between a tyrannical head and his discontented subjects. This guard is the embittered person, venting his anger on the nearest defenseless person, perhaps in order to gain a bit of favor with his superiors. Jesus could have accepted it in silence, but he prefers to do something more and says, "Look into yourself. Why did you strike me? What are the roots of your action? If they are good, I am ready to let myself be struck; but if there is

no well-founded reason, why are you doing this? Why this dissatisfaction, why this bitterness and frustration? What is the
matter with you?" In other words, Jesus accomplishes a work of
evangelization and liberation in his encounter with a person
whom he has never seen before and will never see again, one
who has offended him by humiliating him in public. Jesus does
not react with a disdainful silence but with the active patience
by which he *is* gospel and *is* the Word of God, given to that person to the end, without reserve. Jesus is truly the prophet who
delivers himself up to humanity totally.

The Death of Moses and the Death of Jesus

In this meditation we shall consider the final details of Moses' life, which will in turn aid us to clarify and better understand the meaning of Jesus' death and hence of Mary's death and our own. At each of these four levels of our meditation we shall dwell on a number of texts. Originally I intended to entitle this meditation: "The Death of Moses and the Death of Jesus; the Death of Mary and the Death of the Christian." But I prefer to speak of Mary's Pasch, her Passover. And so it seems fitting to treat also of the Christian's Pasch, our Passover. In any event, the paschal theme permeates our entire meditation.

Let us approach our task with the prayer that always reminds us of the hour of our death:

> Hail Mary, full of grace, the Lord is with thee;
> blessed art thou among women,
> and blessed is the fruit of thy womb, Jesus.
> Holy Mary, Mother of God, pray for us sinners,
> now and at the hour of our death. Amen.

1. Moses' Death

Now we turn our attention to the death of Moses as it is described in chapters 31, 32 and 34 of Deuteronomy. It is interesting to note how much space is devoted to recounting this death, much more than for other prophets such as Isaiah or Jeremiah, concerning whose deaths we know nothing. In comparison, we know much about Moses' death.

Let us first read a few verses from Deuteronomy:

> Moses went and spoke to all Israel as follows, "Today, I am one hundred and twenty years old, and can no longer act as leader. Yahweh has told me, 'You shall not cross this Jordan.' Yahweh your God himself will lead you across, he himself will destroy and dispossess these nations confronting you; Joshua too will lead you across, as Yahweh has said. Yahweh will treat them as he treated Sihon and Og the Amorite kings and their country—he destroyed them. Yahweh will put them at your mercy, and you will deal with them exactly as prescribed by the commandments which I have laid down for you. Be strong, stand firm, have no fear, do not be afraid of them, for Yahweh your God is going with you; he will not fail you or desert you."
>
> Moses then summoned Joshua and, in the presence of all Israel, said to him, "Be strong, stand firm; you will be the one to go with this people into the country which Yahweh has sworn to their ancestors that he would give them; you are to be the one who puts them into possession of it. Yahweh himself will lead you; he will be with you; he will not fail you or desert you. Have no fear, do not be alarmed" (Dt 31:1-8).

Moses Is Not Indispensable

What kind of Moses is before us here? The first thing that strikes me is the honesty with which Moses recognizes that the time of passivity has arrived for him: "I can no longer work! I cannot come and go anymore; I am no longer able to govern." And knowing that he cannot continue, he divests himself of his prerogatives with great freedom: "The Lord will lead you; Joshua will lead you."

How else could Moses have acted? He could have insisted: "Actually I am still strong. I feel fit and am holding my own.

Besides, if I am not around, what will the people do? I want to stay with them and accompany them, for great dangers are threatening them." Instead, Moses is free and detached. He says: "I will not be with you any longer, but you will get along very well without me. With the Lord as your guide, you will win great victories. Greater than those you would have had with me. This man whom I am leaving to you, Joshua, is strong, good and courageous. Have confidence in him." Notice that he does not say of Joshua, as often happens in similar cases, "He is not capable; he has no experience. How will he fare? I have to be near him." Moses, who has been patiently educated to regard his work as the work of God, is now willing to see this work proceed without him, so that its being God's work will be even more evident. On this occasion also Moses shows himself to be the servant of the people by exercising a ministry of consolation: "Take courage, keep calm, and everything will go well. The Lord will be with you."

Now let us read a passage in which Moses' death is described in more detail:

> Yahweh spoke to Moses that same day and said to him, "Climb this mountain of the Abarim, Mount Nebo, in the country of Moab, opposite Jericho, and view the Canaan which I am giving to the Israelites as their domain. Die on the mountain you have climbed, and be gathered to your people, as your brother Aaron died on Mount Hor and was gathered to his people. Because, with the other Israelites, you broke faith with me at the Waters of Meribah-Kadesh in the desert of Zin, because you did not make my holiness clear to the Israelites; you may only see the country from outside; you cannot enter it—the country which I am giving to the Israelites" (Dt 32:48-52).

Then after the lengthy blessing that Moses, the man of God, gives to the tribes of Israel one by one, the actual description of his death finally appears:

Then, leaving the Plains of Moab, Moses went up Mount
Nebo, the peak of Pisgah opposite Jericho, and Yahweh
showed him the whole country: Gilead as far as Dan, the
whole of Naphtali . . . .Yahweh said to him, "This is the
country which I promised on oath to give to Abraham,
Isaac and Jacob, saying: I shall give it to your descendants.
I have allowed you to see it for yourself, but you will not
cross into it."

There in the country of Moab, Moses, servant of Yahweh, died as Yahweh decreed; they buried him in the val-
ley, in the country of Moab, opposite Beth-Peor; but to this
day no one has ever found his grave. Moses was a hundred
and twenty years old when he died, his eye undimmed, his
vigour unimpaired (Dt 34:1-7).

A Scandalous Death

From this description of Moses' death I gather at least three
basic aspects: it is a death in *loneliness*, in *obedience* and in *suffering*.

It is certainly a *lonely* death. Moses does not die among the
people but far from those whom he had loved so much and for
whom he had been literally consumed before God. Now he is
there, all alone on the mountain, without witnesses, and he dies
alone, worn out, spent as it were, from the service he has fulfilled.

Then too, Moses dies in *obedience*, as the text so simply
states: "Moses, servant of Yahweh, died as Yahweh decreed."
He is the only biblical figure of whom it is said that he died this
way: Yahweh commanded, and he died!

Finally, he dies in *suffering*. Note how insistently the text repeats, "You will not see; you will not enter." And with extreme
humility as well as with sorrow, Moses has to accept his situation. In a certain sense he sacrifices himself for all the others:
They will see, but he bears their sin. Actually, as we have seen,
the sin was probably more theirs than his. It was the others who
made him go so far as to lack confidence in Yahweh. He let

100

himself be carried away by his mercy and compassion for the people. Now he bears this sin of the others and consents to expiate it.

Moses, therefore, dies alone, obedient and suffering. No one even knows where he is buried, so that his relatives might come to mourn him. This death is scandalous. Moses does not leave us in peace, even in the way he died. We have never imagined that a leader could die in such estrangement and so completely forsaken.

Moses Disappears

But there is still something else to be said. The fact is that in addition to Moses' death, I gather from this text what I call the *disappearance* of Moses. On the basis of the biblical text we can verify that Moses disappeared from the earth not only in the sense that he was buried in a foreign land — an abominable thing for a Hebrew — or that his burial place was unknown — likewise very painful for an Israelite — but in the sense of his literally disappearing among his own people. It is a curious fact that outside the Pentateuch Moses is scarcely mentioned in the Hebrew Bible again. It is as though he disappears from scripture. He lets himself be deleted, like a servant who has completed his service, which is now passed on to others and has no need of glorious commemorations. It is noteworthy that the prophets hardly ever quote Moses, and the other historical books rarely speak of him. I have often counted the times that he is mentioned, and notwithstanding the immense importance we can attribute to this man, he seems almost to have vanished from Israel's memory. The psalms, too, in which the names of so many personages of Israel appear, mention Moses very seldom. The Book of Wisdom, which recounts the entire story of the Exodus from Egypt, does not name him even once! He is referred to indirectly in one place without being named. The only book that devotes a few very nice lines to Moses is Sirach, a deutero-canonical writing very close to the time of Christ. But to our great astonishment, this book dedicates at least triple or double the amount of space to Aaron, to whom we have not paid much attention until now. Moses accepted being obliterated from the memory of his people.

It is interesting to note that even in the *Haggadah* of the Pasch, the Hebrew paschal ritual which continually speaks of Egypt and the Exodus, Moses is mentioned perhaps once. Something has occurred that may be defined not as a *damnatio memoriae* but rather as a *cancellatio memoriae*. Another instance is Psalm 135, the grand litany of thanksgiving. This psalm enumerates all the great deeds of creation and salvation history. "He alone works wonders. . . . In wisdom he made the heavens. . . . He struck down the first-born of Egypt . . . with a mighty hand and outstretched arm. . . . He split the Sea of Reeds in two . . . Let Israel pass through the middle . . . And drowned Pharaoh and all his army. . . . He led his people through the desert." Not a word about Moses! It is God who has done all this for his people. Moses is hidden in God's arm.

But Moses Remains

There is still a third comment to be made on this point. In reality there are also aspects of the biblical text that indicate a mysterious *permanence* of Moses. We shall consider some of them, beginning with the more conspicuous and proceeding to the more subtle ones.

There is, for instance, the permanence of the books of Moses—the Law, the Pentateuch. Moses remains in the sense that his books remain. Up to the present, Judaism, which ascribes a sacred value to all the books of scripture, distinguishes in fact between the books of Moses and the others. In every synagogue, for example, at the bottom of the bookcase, behind the veil, the books of Moses are kept, but not the other parts of scripture. The former are regarded as sacred books par excellence. There exists, therefore, an objective permanence of

Moses — not personal, triumphalistic or pharaonic, but connected with facts, things and the type of service that he rendered and by which he perdures in Israel. And, if you wish, he also remains close to Christians.

But there is an aspect even more subtle, which I would not have noticed had not the writings of Gregory of Nyssa called it to my attention. Gregory asks himself the meaning of the following words, which we have already heard: "Moses was a hundred and twenty years old when he died, his eye undimmed, his vigour unimpaired." He remarks: "He was very well, then. But what does this mean — a dead man who does not close his eyes, a dead man whose vigor persists?" The rabbis have also posed this question, and their answer could be summarized as follows:

> Moses did not want to die, because he was still very healthy, but God said to him, "You must die." When he resisted, God said, "You will go on living, but Joshua will become your master and the master of all your people." Moses agreed, but immediately afterward he retracted and pleaded, "Let me die, because it is better to die a thousand deaths than to live for an instant in jealousy."

Moses could not have endured such a situation. That is how the rabbis envision it. Gregory of Nyssa's view impresses me as being much more profound. He reads these texts in the light of Christianity and explains: "What does the story say? That Moses, the servant of God, died at the command of Yahweh, that no one knew where his tomb was, that his eyes did not dim nor his countenance shrivel." And he continues:

> From this we learn that, after having passed through so many labors, he was judged worthy to be called by the sublime name of servant of God, which is equivalent to being superior to all. Indeed, anyone who has not transcended all the things of this world cannot serve God. And for him, this is likewise the goal of a virtuous life. The end attained by a virtuous life—made so by the word of God — the end which history calls death is in reality a living death. This

103

death is not followed by burial; no tomb is erected on it; it
does not bring blindness to the eyes nor decomposition to
the features.

To sum up, Moses dies; but as servant of Yahweh he dies in a
way that gives us to understand that he lives. In him the spirit of
the resurrection is mysteriously manifested. It seems that Gregory meant, "One who is a servant of God does die, but life
will be made visible in him." There is a mysterious permanence
of Moses which we cannot quite call resurrection but which is,
nevertheless, oriented to the resurrection of the Servant of Yahweh.

2. The Death of Jesus

Now we shall dwell a moment on the death of Jesus, simply
underlining the aspects that render it both like and unlike the
death of Moses.

First of all, Jesus is abandoned to *loneliness*. In Mark's gospel
we see that when the soldiers came to seize him, the disciples
"all deserted him and fled" (Mk 14:50). This is a much more
bitter loneliness than that of Moses, for Moses withdrew from
the people on his own, while here the disciples shamefully desert Jesus at a decisive moment. Jesus is left alone, or rather,
abandoned.

Like Moses, Jesus lives this loneliness in *obedience*, even to
dying consumed by service, "emptied" by service, as Paul says:

But he emptied himself, . . .
even to accepting death on a cross (Phil 2:8).

Jesus is the image of the self-emptying servant who is delivered
up to God without reserve.

Jesus also dies *suffering*. Moses was unable to enter the Promised Land, but the rabbis interpreted this as an act of God's
mercy because the many difficulties that awaited him would have

disillusioned him! Therefore the Lord decided to have him die while he was still seeing the land from a distance. Jesus, on the contrary, dies in the sorrow of one who is rejected by those to whom he came with open heart, ready to give all. Here we can recall the words of John:

> He came to his own
>> and his own people did not accept him (Jn 1:11).

We have just presented the parallels between the death of Jesus and that of Moses. Nevertheless, how much more tragic, painful and humiliating is the death of Jesus, how much more the result of human malice, of the inability of humanity to love Love!

The Disappearance of Jesus

We may likewise speak of a *disappearance* of Jesus, an extinction of Jesus analogous to that of Moses. Actually, we are accustomed to think of Jesus' death and resurrection together. But the resurrection is not an escape from death; rather, it is the power of God poured out on him who has entered into death totally, submitting just like any of us to its power to annihilate. Death is the end of everything — of dreams, hopes, friendships and the possibility of living.

I believe that we all experience death in this way within our own psychic life, even if we face death in faith, hope and love. The pneumatic life of the Spirit gives us hope, but psychic life gives us evidence of the end. Jesus consented to letting this evidence of the end be visible in him; hence he experienced his death as real death, not merely as a passage but as the end, as destruction, as the annihilation of life. For this reason also, Jesus is the first among the dead, the one who for our sake entered death first, so that we might overcome the fear of death. Jesus' death is, therefore, a real death and as such is inconsolable. The Father, however, proclaims to us that Jesus, who casts

105

himself into this death trusting in the Father's word, lives in glory.

In conclusion, in contrast to the feeble permanence of Moses — barely suggested by the allusion to the eyes that do not fail, the absence of a tomb and the vigor of his countenance — there is the risen and living Jesus who appears to his disciples reassuring them, "Do not be afraid. It is I!" The experience of Moses gives way to an experience entirely new, unforeseen and completely different — the experience of the resurrection. In reference to Moses, scripture tells us something about the resurrection, but with a timidity that only the power of Christ is able to raise up.

3. Mary's Pasch

After Jesus, Mary is the first to have made the paschal experience of passage from this life to the life of glory. This is the mystery of her assumption into heaven. But how can we contemplate Mary's Pasch if scripture does not speak of it?

I believe that there is, nevertheless, a means of contemplating Mary's Pasch. Therefore I shall suggest some texts that help us understand Mary's passage from this life and her entrance into glory. Regarding the passage from this life, Paul says, "We are full of confidence, then, and long instead to be exiled from the body and to be at home with the Lord" (2 Cor 5:8). In addition, "Life to me, of course, is Christ, but then death would be a positive gain. . . . I am caught in this dilemma: I want to be gone and to be with Christ, and this is by far the stronger desire. . . " (Phil 1:21,23). I see in these words Mary's sentiments — her desire to be with Christ, to leave earthy experience behind, so that the final experience, the fullness of vision, may be revealed in her.

The presence of this desire in Mary means that Jesus has already overcome in her the fear of death. As the Letter to the Hebrews states:

> Since all the *children* share the same human nature, he too shared equally in it, so that by his death he could set aside him who held the power of death, namely the devil, and set free all those who had been held in slavery all their lives by the fear of death (Heb 2:14-15).

This is a very important concept. According to Hebrews, sin is the result of slavery to the conditionings to which the Pharaoh subjects us. Why are we subservient to these conditionings? Because we are afraid of death. Basically, every sin is an expression of our fear of death, inasmuch as it represents a form of unhealthy possession of something that we do not want to let go. Actually, this thing, whatever it is, constitutes a sign of life for us, so that if we lose possession of it we would feel overcome by death. Consequently, every form of possessiveness, unbridled pleasure, wealth and exploitation of others, everything to which we are in any way attached with morbid and possessive inclination can be summarized in one cry: "I do not want to die! I want to be sure that I do not die but go on living." Therefore Hebrews says that Jesus, having been the first to pass through death, frees us from the fear of death and from every tyranny to which we are subject. In dying, Mary makes her own the words of Paul; she has been fully liberated from the fear of death and now beholds Christ as her final fulfillment.

I suggest another text in connection with Mary's entrance into glory, one that could be used for the feast of her assumption:

> "Come, you whom my Father has blessed, take as your heritage the kingdom prepared for you since the foundation of the world. For I was hungry and you gave me food, I was thirsty and you gave me drink" (Mt 25:34-35).

Mary was the first to comprehend that God's word can be concealed in such a tiny reality as a child, and that in serving this reality the fullness or totality of the word of God is attained.

Mary intuited the whole in the part, so that in serving the Child Jesus as well as in serving the little group of the first Christians, she served all of humanity. Her heart was capable of opening up to every creature, and this qualified her to be mother of the church, not only of the church that now is, but of that which ought to be and will be — of all humankind.

4. The Paschs of the Christian

In the caption, I deliberately used the plural — *Paschs* of the Christian — not solely because being inserted in time we celebrate a new Pasch, a new Easter, each year and find ourselves each Easter in a different situation from that of the previous year, but also because different kinds of Paschs take place in us. I shall mention three of them.

The Pasch of Christian Baptism

In the first place, there is the fundamental Pasch, which is the passage through the Sea of Reeds, the *Pasch of Christian baptism*. This must be renewed each day, for while it remains substantially something that has happened in the past, it still has to be integrated into our life. Once and for all we have passed from death to life, from possessiveness to the giving of ourselves, from a pharaonic apostolate to an apostolate of service. By now it is an acquired value that we must continually renew in reference to our baptism. Jesus has taken us by the hand, has made us pass on dry ground through the Sea of Reeds and has saved us.

The Passage From Activity to Passivity

Then there is a second Pasch, the one Moses experienced in the final days of his life, which consists in *passing from activity to passivity*. It is a passage that can be traumatic, but all of us have to pass through it in one way or another. We want to do

things, we are made to do things, our thinking is oriented to doing, we make plans, we want to serve others. But the time will
come when we are predominantly the object of the actions of
others — the time of sickness, which becomes a true and real
Pasch of sickness, the prelude to the *Pasch of death*. These are
the two Paschs that we still await. Day by day we are living this
passage from activity to passivity. It is useless to stop the hands
of the clock or refuse to turn the pages of the calendar; we are
on the way to passivity. And we know — one more clearly than
another — how painful, humiliating and purifying these passivi-
ties are.

Sickness entails being more passive than active; it means not
serving but being served. We would like to serve, but for all of
us the time comes when we have to allow ourselves to be served
and accept being served. At times we can witness real inner
tragedies in people who cannot endure being a burden to others
after having heroically spent themselves all their life. They find
it difficult to accept the gift that others offer for them. Since this
will be a really new experience for us, we ought to prepare ourselves for it. When the Lord comes to meet us, it will be like a
new passage through the Sea of Reeds. It may be an illness
properly speaking, which confines us to bed and renders us
helpless and completely dependent on the services of others, or
it may be the little inabilities that we carry around with us,
which prevent us from accomplishing so many things, so that
we need the help of others. We have to realize that in fact we are
never purely active but are a mixture of activity and passivity —
thank God, because this state of affairs renders mutual service
possible. In this blend of activity and passivity, activity predom-
inates as long as we have good health, then the equilibrium
gradually shifts in favor of passivity, until the Lord calls us, not
to total passivity but to return our spirit to him. This is the definitive passivity through which Moses and Jesus passed — and
Mary too in some way — and through which we shall certainly
have to pass.

The Pasch of death is the touchstone of our entire life. In saying this I am not referring, however, to the death that we shall actually die, for none of us can program his or her own death, with the exception of the suicide, who thereby commits an act of violence, a breach of trust against God. In this regard we can only ask for the grace to serve God, which includes offering him whatever death will be ours, despite all the contrary suggestions that come from today's world. The death that I have in mind now is the one which is already within us, namely, the thought of death and the fear of death. The reflections that we can make in this regard vary greatly from one person to another. My own impression is that whenever I find myself faced with the real possibility of death — or even imagine it as real — I feel sheer rebellion against this possibility, to the point that I perceive clearly how only the power of faith, hope and charity will permit me to accept it without despairing. On the other hand I see that I cannot program this hope, precisely because it entails facing a restricted, non-programmable situation that no one can prepare in advance at all, given the absolute uniqueness of the structures proper to it. It is precisely here that we place all our confidence in God. We can say, "I can program my schedule today. I hope that I shall not lose my faith nor my head, because I more or less foresee what will happen to me today." But if my situation suddenly changes and I find myself confronted with a tragic, unprovided, unforeseen and unwanted death, an attack of rage and desperation can rise up and threaten to overcome me. Then only God's grace and powerful mercy, Jesus' death for me and Mary's death, which conquered the fear of death, can help me. Therefore I understand why the church likes to have us pray many times a day, "pray for us now and at the hour of our death." This hour is indeed truly decisive, in the sense that it calls us to the harvest, so that we may finally reap the value of all the other hours that we have lived in the course of our existence. "After this exile, show us the blessed fruit of thy womb: Jesus!"

The Pasch of the Resurrection

The third Pasch is that of the resurrection, which we both live now and still await. We live it because the Spirit of the Risen Lord already lives in us. Hence we have already passed from death to life, and this has important consequences for our entire moral, ascetical and spiritual life, for our very anthropology. Christian anthropology is that of a being who has risen. "The Spirit of him who raised Jesus from the dead has made his home in you," says Paul; and if so, "he who raised Christ Jesus from the dead will give life to your own mortal bodies through his Spirit living in you" (Rom 8:11).

We live by dint of this resurrection which has already begun and is the pledge of our hope in what awaits us. From this, Paul draws the conclusion:

> So then, my brothers, we have no obligation to human na-
> ture to be dominated by it. If you do live in that way, you
> are doomed to die; but if by the Spirit you put to death the
> habits originating in the body, you will have life (Rom
> 8:12 13).

Then in Galatians, after having enumerated the works of the body, which lead to death, he lists those of the Spirit: "Love, joy, peace, patience, kindness, goodness, trustfulness, gentleness and self-control" (Gal 5:22). This is the paschal life of the Christian. Let us conclude by praying "Come, Lord Jesus!" In other words, "Lord, already in us, come powerfully within us and, this very day, make us live a paschal life." Only thus can we face our death in hope, joy and even with desire, as Mary did. This is something incredible for people of this world, but wonderful for those who await the resurrection.

Moses and the People

For this final meditation I have taken inspiration from Mary of Magdala. At first we might wonder what Mary of Magdala has to do with Moses. Originally I had thought of a mediation on the "Sacraments of Moses." By this expression I mean, for example, the water from the rock, the passover supper, the bread from heaven — all elements that share in the sacramental life of the people of God in the desert and, taken up again in the New Testament, especially in John, become images of the sacramental life of the Christian community. I had also thought of some considerations on "The Prayer of Moses," using various passages from Exodus. In the end, for this meditation on the connection between Moses and Jesus, I preferred to draw inspiration from the scene of the meeting between Jesus and Mary of Magdala. Together we shall see the reasons for this.

1. Moses, the Man of Big Numbers

First of all, I would like to take a quick glance at the relationship between Moses and the people, at the same time keeping in mind the relationship that Jesus experienced with the people. In all his undertakings Moses seems to be the man of *big numbers*, and not merely because he wrote the Book of Numbers in which so many large numbers appear. We read, for instance, in the data on the first census: "The total of these for the tribe of Reuben was forty-six thousand five hundred . . . for the tribe of Simeon was fifty-nine thousand three hundred . . . for the tribe of Gad was forty-five thousand six hundred and fifty" (Nm 1:21,23,25). Finally, it concludes: "All the Israelites of twenty years and over, fit to bear arms, were counted by families. Altogether, the total came to six hundred and three thousand five hundred and fifty" (Nm 1:45-46). Even aside from these specific texts, however, Moses remains the man of big numbers, because in general he had contact only with the multitudes.

In this regard Jesus was very different, for he always had a relatively limited audience. When the gospel does speak of a large crowd, it does not mean that a whole people was subject to Jesus or that a group as such claimed his main interest. I have found only one episode regarding Moses that could be called evangelical in the sense of a simple encounter between two persons. It was when Moses was on his way back to Egypt, after that bad night in which he nearly died:

> Yahweh said to Aaron, "Go into the desert to meet Moses." So he went, and met him at the mountain of God and kissed him. Moses then told Aaron all that Yahweh had said when sending him and all the signs he had ordered him to perform (Ex 4:27-28).

This little scene in which Moses and Aaron embrace in the desert and converse quietly together is the only evangelical scene in the whole story of Moses, the sole instance of a one-to-one meeting. In every other case Moses deals with the masses or with representatives of a large body: with Pharaoh as representative of all Egypt, or with Aaron as representative of Israel. Right after this scene which I have called evangelical Moses turns to all the people:

> Moses and Aaron then went and gathered all the elders of the Israelites together, and Aaron repeated everything that Yahweh had said to Moses, and in the sight of the people performed the signs. The people were convinced (Ex 4:29-31).

114

Rapport has been resumed with the masses; Moses, by way of Aaron, makes contact with the people.

To confirm what we have said, I shall cite still another passage, occurring after the crossing of the Sea of Reeds:

> Moses and Aaron then said to the whole community of Israelites, "This evening you will know that it was Yahweh who brought you out of Egypt, and tomorrow morning you will see the glory of Yahweh, for Yahweh has heard your complaints about him. What are we, that your complaint should be against us?" (Ex 16:6-7).

In a later passage, it could appear as though Moses were dealing with one or two people in a rather interpersonal relationship, whereas in reality he is conferring with the artists of the sanctuary; "Moses then summoned Bezalel, Oholiah and all the skilled men whose hearts Yahweh had endowed with skill" (Ex 36:2). Here too, Moses calls not merely one or two persons but all the artists and gives them instructions and the necessary money.

Hence I believe we can state that Moses represents in a very strict sense the principle of efficiency on the social, structural and hierarchical levels, applied to the people of God. And Moses dedicated himself untiringly to applying this principle. Scarcely an evangelical incident of merciful contact with individuals is written of him. He does not meet a widow of Naim or cure a leper. Moses never speaks with a centurion or cures Peter's mother-in-law. He does not engage in discussion with the moneychanger Levi and call him to be a disciple. Moses never pays a friendly visit to the house of Lazarus, Martha and Mary, nor does he cure a Bartimaeus. Since he has so many extraordinary things to do, Moses has no time for individual and personal situations. Moses has no friends; he is always occupied with matters on the general, universal, global level.

2. Jesus and Mary of Magdala

Jesus is a person who has both time and friends. A typical case is the meeting between Jesus and Mary of Magdala:

> But Mary was standing outside near the tomb, weeping. Then, as she wept, she stooped to look inside, and saw two angels in white sitting where the body of Jesus had been, one at the head, the other at the feet. They said, "Woman, why are you weeping?" "They have taken my Lord away," she replied, "and I don't know where they have put him." As she said this she turned round and saw Jesus standing there, though she did not realise that it was Jesus. Jesus said to her, "Woman, why are you weeping? Who are you looking for?" Supposing him to be the gardener, she said, "Sir, if you have taken him away, tell me where you have put him, and I will go and remove him." Jesus said, "Mary!" She turned round then and said to him in Hebrew, "Rabbuni!" — which means Master. Jesus said to her, "Do not cling to me, because I have not yet ascended to the Father. But go and find my brothers, and tell them: I am ascending to my Father and your Father, to my God and your God" (Jn 20:11-17).

In this, as in innumerable other gospel passages, Jesus exercises the role of consoler. If Moses is the man of big numbers, Jesus is the *man of small numbers*. He takes one person or another at a time; he stops to chat; he waits until the other understands, until the person undergoes a process of purification and can finally open his or her eyes and see. We might well ask why the Lord wastes so much time with Mary of Magdala. Why does he wait until she matures, sees and understands? Why does he not immediately say who he is? Jesus gives her time. The same thing happens with the two disciples from Emmaus. He first spends almost two hours in accompanying them, then listens to them to let their anguish surface and to enlighten them. At last there is the supper. How much time he squanders while the whole world is waiting for him to reveal his resurrection! The apostles are in tears, Peter is still bewildered, the good people in Jerusalem are grieving and thinking now everything is at an end. It is all very strange.

The fact is that here we see the logic of the lost sheep. The ninety-nine are there waiting, but he goes looking for the one straggler. It is the logic of the lost coin, of the attention bestowed on the son who does not work instead of on the son who is productive, the mysterious logic of God's particularization. God seems to get lost in the individual, willingly concealing himself in the most minute and most simple things, in the things for which we have neither the time nor the leisure that would enable us to attend to them. We are tempted to assert that, in cases concerning an entire group, the group should be cared for. Jesus, however, says, "The group can wait. I am attending to this particular person."

In conclusion, Moses has neither time nor friends whereas Jesus has both. This is the difference between the Mosaic law and the gospel.

3. The Word Makes Itself Small

Now I shall comment on two very compact and meaningful expressions used by the Fathers of the church: *o logos brachynetai*, "the word becomes small"; and *o logos pachynetai*, "the word becomes opaque."

Let us reflect a bit on these expressions. What is the *logos*? In the Johannnine sense the *logos* is the supreme and universal manifestation of the Father, the most perfect revelation of God. It is God speaking of himself. Hence the *logos* expresses the characteristics of the Father: wisdom, universality, omnipotence, omniscience . . . . This *logos* is the one in whom everything has been created: the universe, humanity, things, historical situations. According to the Greek mentality *logos* could also be understood as "the reason for everything." Moses asked,

"Why does the bush not burn up?" This question, which came from the *pneuma* — the Spirit — was already directing him to the *logos*. The *logos* is the locus in which all questions are resolved and from which all questions proceed in order to break into the human heart. It is preeminently the locus of universality, where unconditional desire to understand is rooted and where this same desire can attain its terminus. It is the locus in which all human beings created in the *logos* can understand, comprehend, know and love one another. In brief, simplifying the terms to some extent, the *logos* is the *ratio universalis*, the reason for everything. Therefore the *logos* subtly penetrates everywhere and is the supreme universal unifier, since it confers on all things the meaning of their differences and similarities and at the same time of their convergences. This is how the Book of Wisdom describes it.

Hence the scandal on which the Greek Fathers meditated: *o logos brachynetai*. This universal Word makes itself small, it contracts into time and space, so that it is here and not there, it is here now but was not here before, it is here now but not tomorrow. It makes itself small and in so doing makes itself particular and therefore accessible. It adapts itself to an interpersonal relationship, to that relationship which touches each individual, and thus participates in the particularity of the person. In this way it can encounter each one in a unique and absolute manner.

So that we may understand all this better, I shall try to clarify it with some examples. In Exodus we find that Moses was practically the only one who had a personal relationship with God: "Yahweh would talk to Moses face to face, as a man talks to his friend" (Ex 33:11). Likewise, after the rebellion of Miriam and Aaron the Lord says of Moses:

> to him I speak face to face,
>> plainly and not in riddles,
>> and he sees Yahweh's form (Ex 12:8).

This extraordinary familiarity between Moses and God, almost unique in history, will be remembered in all the traditions to come. Sirach praises Moses by saying that God "gave him the commandments face to face" (Sir 45:6). This face-to-face relationship was reserved to Moses alone; everyone else made contact with God through Moses. After the proclamation of the Decalogue, we read:

> Seeing the thunder pealing, the lightning flashing, the trumpet blasting and the mountain smoking, the people were all terrified and kept their distance. "Speak to us yourself," they said to Moses, "and we will obey; but do not let God speak to us, or we shall die" (Ex 20:18-19).

This rule remains valid during the whole of Moses' time.

But when the *logos* is revealed in Christ, it makes itself small, not only because it assumes a physical dimension that it did not have before, but especially because it becomes particular, a part of history. However scandalous this might seem, the Fathers of the church were not afraid to affirm it in saying that this brilliant Word, which could shoot through the world like an arrow and enlighten hearts, suddenly became opaque — earthbound — and insignificant (*o logos pachynetai*).

This opacity of the Word is scandalous to us too, for with our tenaciously pagan religiosity we are always looking for a sign from heaven, visible to all and universal. Or with our irreducibly philosophical mentality, we want to encapsulate God in the nets of our mind, in the nets of our grand phenomenological or sociological laws that govern religious manifestations. We would like a God whom everyone could understand in the same way, because he would reveal himself to everyone in the same way and in an instantaneous flash enlighten the minds of all peoples of all times. But it so happens that this God, about whom we think we know everything, makes himself like a tiny fish before this terrible net with which we aspire to entangle the divinity in a circle in which everything is predetermined, and he slips

119

through the mesh of the net. He makes himself small in order to be free, to be himself. Indeed, it pertains to God to become small without being constrained by this littleness. Conversely, however great our ideas of God may be, he is always greater than these ideas.

God is small and great at the same time, and he eludes all our attempts to program our dialogue with him. God is love, and love does not let itself be programmed. God becomes small and frustrates our programs; he accepts being a scandal to all those who do not want to leave him free to love us as he wishes, with a love that is true, that is, unforeseeable, inventive, ardent, tender, jealous, incendiary. It is a love that no one can control, because it is the secret with which God loves.

It is this love that the small Jesus, the *logos*-become-small, offers to Mary of Magdala, the two disciples of Emmaus and the apostles, "wasting" his time with them. In this way God's love repeatedly disconcerts us in our pagan nostalgia for a revelation that is complete, total, absolute, definitive and always under our control. The God of the gospel, the God of true love is ever surprising and upsetting us. Even in every true human relationship, when the power of love is released, unforeseeable things are continually brought to light. We think we understand a person, whereas in reality we understand nothing, for a thousand new revelations can erupt like a volcano. God cannot be put under a gauge to determine his where, how and when, because he does not operate in regular forms and figures but in eruptions. This is the God of the Bible, from beginning to end. Throughout the pages of scripture, from Moses to Jesus, we are incessantly put into contact with this God. But we would rather not surrender to this truth about God. The fact remains, however, that only this truth about God allows us to encounter him on an I-thou basis, to discover that not only do we know him but we are truly known as we are, in our unrepeatable selves that no one else knows, in our uniqueness that no human being can fathom to its depths.

120

4. The Risen Jesus

Who is this risen Jesus? It is the Jesus made small unto death, made opaque unto scandal, even to becoming the most despised of the despised. Therefore God enables him to become a presence both universal and particular to each and all. The resurrection of Jesus is not identical with the return of Jesus to the world in general; rather, it actualizes Jesus' power to be present in the Spirit to each and to all.

Let us now dwell on the expressions "present" and "to each and all." The risen Jesus is present to each one, as though the individual loved person were the only object of his love. The risen Christ is the love of God revealed in our hearts by the Spirit, in the heart of each and of all and in each of all. Jesus does not individualize this "each"; he gives himself to the church, the world, the angels, the universe. Jesus exists for all. But he is for all in such a way that he is for each one, thus making each one become a part of the whole. Such is the power of the resurrection of the "abbreviated" Word, which has made itself small. Whoever accepts the scandal of the Word-become-small will share in the glory of the universality of the cosmic Word which embraces and synthesizes everything, in which all things find their order and fullness, in which everything is resumed and established.

Now we can understand that very bold statement of Paul, which I would never dare to express if it were not in scripture:

> When everything has been subjected to him, then the Son himself will be subjected to the One who has subjected everything to him, so that God may be all in all (1 Cor 15:28).

I do not find it so difficult to understand that God could be somehow *in all*, but it is more difficult to comprehend his being *all* in all. This is the exact opposite of the particularization of the Incarnation in which God was fully in Jesus; now God becomes *the* fullness, he is fully in all.

Along the way of the scandal of Jesus' particularization until the funereal opacity of the cross, the glory of God totally fills every being. The more I think about it, the more truly grandiose and almost incredible this truth seems to me — that God fills every being with himself. He gives himself, not merely a little but in full. This divine fullness transforms into a divinized totality the entire universe of the human will, which the Son has won for the Father. Though it is true that here we do not yet have the "all in all" that is the final perfection which we are to attain, nevertheless by lovingly contemplating God in all of us, we already obtain a glimpse of how the fullness of God is gradually actuating the "all in all," according to the measure in which each one is able to accept such a vision.

What, then, are the consequences for us, if the risen Jesus becomes a universal and particular presence in each one and in all? The gospel is very concrete about this. Let us turn to Matthew, who perhaps best of all understood and vigorously expresses the consequences of what Jesus risen and present in his church means. Jesus has just said, "I was hungry and you gave me food. I was thirsty and you gave me drink. I was a stranger and you made me welcome, lacking clothes and you clothed me, . . . sick . . . in prison . . . ." Then the upright ask, "But when did we see . . . ?" and receive the reply, "Insofar as you did this" — not to the masses, to the vague totality but — "to *one* of the least of these brothers of mine, you did it to me!" (Mt 25:35,39,40). Anyone who carries to its final consequences the particularization of Jesus will sit at his right hand when he comes in his glory.

Jesus takes time gladly to be with the individual for he knows how to see the "all" in each individual. Matthew has anticipated this politics of the individual who contains the "all": "But anyone who is the downfall of *one* of these little ones who have faith in me would be better drowned in the depths of the sea with a great millstone round his neck" (Mt 18:6). Matthew does not generically warn against giving scandal, but affirms that our destiny is at stake in our relationship with even *one* person. Then too: "See that you never despise *any* of these little ones, for I tell you that their angels in heaven are continually in the presence of my Father in heaven" (Mt 18:10). And at the conclusion of the brief parable of the lost sheep: "Suppose a man has a hundred sheep and one of them strays; will he not leave the ninety-nine on the hillside and go in search of the stray? In truth I tell you, if he finds it, it gives him more joy than do the ninety-nine that did not stray at all. Similarly, it is never the will of your Father in heaven that one of these little ones should be lost" (Mt 18:12-14, emphasis added). Here we see the incarnational particularization of God in Jesus translated into Christian practice. We are called to find God in the world, in things, in others, in history. But this will never be possible if we do not proceed from our immediate situation. In every actual situation, even if it affords the opportunity for only the smallest service, we touch the totality of service; in each fragment we are in contact with the whole of God, who is revealing himself.

We conclude this meditation with the brief prayer that St. Ignatius includes in the *Contemplation for Obtaining Love*:

> Take, Lord, and receive all my liberty, my memory, my understanding and my entire will. All that I am and possess you have given me. I return it all to you, Lord. All is yours, to be disposed of according to your will. Give me your love and grace, and this suffices.